PROGRESSIVE ROCK KEYBOARD

THE COMPLETE GUIDE WITH AUDIO!

T0083935

PLAYBACK+
Speed • Pitch • Balance • Loop

To access audio visit:
www.halleonard.com/mylibrary

4803-4588-7323-8316

INTRODUCTION

Welcome to *Progressive Rock Keyboard*. If you're interested in what makes progressive rock such a unique and special genre for keyboardists, then you've come to the right place! Whatever your experience level, this book will help you play and compose music in various "prog" styles.

Progressive rock possesses a wide variety of special characteristics not often found in "rock 'n' roll," and this book will offer insight into what makes it so unique. If you are interested in playing prog covers, a deeper understanding of the complex musical relationships can enhance your practice and performance of these tunes. If composition is your game, you will find plenty of material on how to compose not only your own prog-sounding keyboard parts, but music for the whole band if you so desire.

In the process, we'll also examine some of the most well-known sub-genres in this style, exploring their diversity. With a deeper knowledge of these sub-styles, you may end up creating your own unique sound as a result.

Six complete tunes in various progressive rock styles are included in the "Style File" chapter at the end of the book. They have been recorded with a real band using some of the most authentic progressive rock keyboard instruments. Transcribed keyboard parts are included for all of these examples.

Good luck with your Progressive Rock Keyboard!

About the Audio

You will find audio demonstrations of many of the musical examples in the book. Most of the tracks feature a full band sound so that you can hear and understand better how the keyboard parts fit in to this context. Please see the individual chapters for specific information on the audio tracks and how to use them.

Musical examples recorded by Dan Maske. "Style File" tunes recorded at eDream Studios, Milwaukee, WI by:

> Dan Maske, keyboards
> William Kopecky, electric bass
> Craig Walkner, drumset
> Angela Schmidt, cello
> Sean Gill, guitar

About the Author

Dan Maske is keyboardist and composer for the Cuneiform Records progressive rock group Far Corner. The ensemble, founded by Maske and his wife Angela Schmidt, has performed at international progressive rock festivals including Progday in North Carolina, and the Orion Sound Studios Progressive Rock Showcase in Baltimore. Please visit *far-corner.com* and *cuneiformrecords.com* for more information. Dan is also a composer of concert music for bands, orchestras, and chamber groups, with several published and recorded compositions. His music has been performed throughout the U.S., as well as in Europe and Asia. Dan holds a doctoral degree in music composition.

CONTENTS

Chapter 1

WHAT IS PROGRESSIVE ROCK?

Progressive rock is a style of rock music that began in the late 1960s. Taking as a foundation from the Beatles' 1967 *Sgt. Pepper's Lonely Hearts Club Band*, many musicians began to push the boundaries of rock music. Part of this push came in the form of applying classical music forms and virtuosity to the compositions; longer songs, mood changes, surprises, and a certain element of drama set this style apart from rock 'n' roll. This music existed more for the true listening experience, rather than serving the role of music for dancing, partying, and rebellion. Lyrics were often about subjects other than love and socializing, and took on science fiction, fantasy, and philosophical themes. Many believe the first true progressive rock album to be *In the Court of the Crimson King*, the 1969 album from King Crimson. Other founding groups that began around the same time include Yes; Emerson, Lake & Palmer (ELP); Genesis; and Jethro Tull. More bands immediately followed, such as Gentle Giant, Kansas, and Rush. These groups attained high levels of popularity, and are probably the best-known. However, many other groups from all over the world had their beginnings in the early '70s, and many new progressive rock bands continue to form, record, and perform—all of which are in no small part responsible for the phenomenon of the genre.

Progressive Rock Sub-Genres

Over the years, the genre has branched out into many different "sub-genres." Though the sub-genres below are clearly defined, one may notice some overlap. No artist simply belongs to only one of these categories, but often combines qualities of several. Prevalent in all progressive rock is a desire to move beyond the accepted mainstream of popular music, and draw heavily upon other styles, all under a "rock" umbrella. Though classical music may dominate as an influence in a large number of groups, many styles from all over the world play a part. The terms below are only some of the most common sub-genre labels. For a complete listing with thorough descriptions, visit *The Gibraltar Encyclopedia of Progressive Rock* online at www.gepr.net.

Symphonic

Most of the founding progressive rock bands from the late '60s–early '70s fall under this category. The term **symphonic** refers to elements such as the use of orchestral instruments and keyboards simulating a large symphonic sound. Classical music forms come into play, with single songs spanning durations longer than twenty minutes—some songs existing as multi-movement works in a direct parallel to classical music. Displays of musical virtuosity are also common in the form of demanding solos, meter changes, shifts in tempo, and mood changes. Some music consists of an expansion and development of the pop rock song. These tunes contained the catchy hooks prevalent in pop music, but sought to develop these hooks and themes further. Though the subgenre saw its heyday in the 1970s, many groups continued in the style, with a renaissance of new bands appearing in the 1990s. Notable founding artists include Yes, Genesis, ELP, King Crimson, PFM, and Banco. Some newer bands include Spock's Beard, Änglagård, and The Flower Kings.

Classical

This sub-genre may be seen as an overlap, or perhaps a more specific focus on an area of symphonic. One of the more distinguishing characteristics includes a stronger, more direct imitation of the compositional techniques found in classical music. The term **classical**, as used in this case, refers more specifically to music before 1900, encompassing the Baroque, Classical, and Romantic periods. Classical music as it was in the twentieth century is often compared to progressive rock in the "Rock In Opposition" subgenre (see next page). In this classical style, music could often sound like that of Mozart, for example, played on rock music instruments. Sometimes, as in the case of ELP, a group would take actual classical compositions and arrange them for rock band. Notable artists include The Nice, ELP, Gentle Giant, Ekseption, and Ars Nova.

Fusion

Often called "jazz rock," **fusion** is more a sub-genre of jazz than progressive rock, with its beginnings stemming from Miles Davis' *Bitches Brew*. The music is largely based on improvised soloing, but includes more composed elements than most jazz. Prominent artists include Soft Machine, Nucleus, Brand X, Niacin, Allan Holdsworth, Mahavishnu Orchestra, Tribal Tech, Tunnels, and Return to Forever.

Neoprogressive

Neoprogressive came about in the early '80s, evolving from the more pop-directed sound of late '70s Genesis. By this time, the progressive rock styles of the early–mid '70s had faded from the mainstream with most of the genre going underground. This "new" progressive rock possessed some of the characteristics of the earlier prog, but was more refined and polished, with a bigger emphasis on hook-driven song structures. Thus, this sub-genre is considered to be the most "audience friendly," not concerned with breaking ground or going to any extremes. One may think of it as progressive-influenced pop rock. Some of the bands from the '70s evolved into a neoprogressive style in the '80s in order to keep up with the times and survive. Bands adopting this idiom include Collage, IQ, Jadis, Marillion, Pallas, Pendragon, and some Rush ('80s–'00s).

Progressive Metal

Progressive metal saw its birth in the 1980s as heavy and speed metal stylings combined with some influence from the classic '70s bands. Bands with a heavier edge like Rush and Deep Purple, along with heavy and speed metal groups like Metallica and Iron Maiden, were of great influence. What often sets progressive metal apart from standard metal is the use of keyboards. Though it is still largely guitar-driven, the keys often take center stage in displays of virtuosity. Notable artists include Dream Theater, Fates Warning, Symphony X, Ayreon, Shadow Gallery, and Pain of Salvation.

Rock In Opposition (RIO)

The term **Rock in Opposition** comes from an organizational movement by five European bands in the late '70s. The "opposition" in this case was to the music industry's demands of compromise over art. These bands chose to create music they were proud of, without regard to marketability. Thus, the music was often adventurous, extending far beyond traditions and conventions of mainstream rock. Compositions covered a wide range in styles from contemporary classical music to avant garde experimentalism. Eventually the movement disbanded, but the term **RIO** persisted, representing the most adventurous side of progressive rock. The original RIO bands were Henry Cow, Univers Zero, Samla Mammas Manna, Stormy Six, and Etron Fou. Next-generation RIO-style bands include Thinking Plague, 5UUs, Sleepytime Gorilla Museum, and Miriodor.

Space Rock

Born in the '60s from the psychedelic stylings of early Pink Floyd, **space rock**'s primary focus was on creating atmosphere. Part of the goal was to create music for sitting down and listening—as opposed to music for dancing, a la rock 'n' roll. This notion played a heavy role in the spawning of progressive rock, which attempted to create "concert works" for listening to, akin to classical music. The difference with space rock was its emphasis on hallucinogenic and surreal imagery, with listening being more of a relaxing, meditative experience. While some of the music may be soothing, other compositions take a more aggressive approach, full of great tension and drama. Heavy use of effects such as delay and reverb are a major part of the spacey sound. Synthesizers representing non-acoustic instruments also play an important role. In addition to Pink Floyd, noteworthy groups include Gong, Hawkwind, Ozric Tentacles, Hidria Spacefolk, Ship of Fools, and Quarkspace.

In the spirit of progessiveness, this book discusses and presents examples from each sub-genre above. So whether you wish to create a big symphonic sound, improvise some tasty solos, add a classical music spice to your playing, forge blistering heavy metal lines, concoct some spacey sonic constellations, or all of the above, you'll be provided with the tools to accomplish these goals.

Chapter 2

KEYBOARD INSTRUMENTS

All kinds of keyboard instruments have been used in progressive rock, from the traditional acoustic piano, to organs, digital synths, and even the accordion. A handful of these instruments helped define the classic progressive rock sound in the late '60s and '70s. Though these instruments faded from use a bit in the 1980s due to the digital synthesizer revolution, they returned in the '90s, and are in use now more than ever. Several of these instruments help give the music that special "prog" sound, and many newer bands have either obtained the traditional vintage instruments, or use samples of them. Some of the most commonly used keyboard instruments are described in this chapter, along with examples in the styles of famous prog tunes that feature them. In creating your own prog-style keyboard parts, if you can't get your hands on one of these vintage instruments, many of the sounds are available in software packages and plug-ins containing sounds true to the originals.

Piano

This instrument needs little introduction. The piano existed long before progressive rock (and rock 'n' roll music in general) and is a staple in both classical and jazz. In progressive rock of the '70s, the instrument was often used in classical-type solos in performances by Rick Wakeman (Yes) and Keith Emerson (ELP), among many others. The piano can be used to "comp" chord progressions, play melodies and bass lines, and serve as a percussion instrument. Due to its percussive quality, the only real limitation is that it cannot sustain pitches—they eventually die away. Yet one of the most unique areas of piano sonorities is revealed when it is used as a kind of percussion instrument, playing accented, staccato notes in the low register. Few other instruments can capture this same quality, and it is great for playing percussive **ostinatos** (repeated short, rhythmic patterns). The following example demonstrates this pianistic quality, which has been used by progressive rock groups such as ELP, helping turn the instrument into something rhythmic and aggressive.

TRACK 1

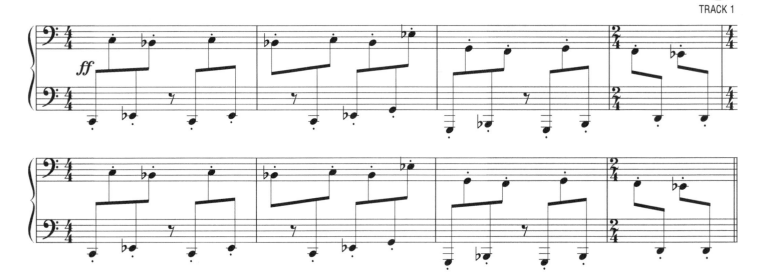

Throughout this book, you will hear many examples utilizing piano, an instrument featured on dozens of the accompanying audio tracks.

Hammond Organ

Though often used in jazz and other pop music, especially that from the '70s, the Hammond organ represents one of the most distinctive sounds in progressive rock.

Today in the early twenty-first century, the organ may sound a bit dated with respect to mainstream music, but in prog, the Hammond sound has endured, and may eventually reach the timeless status of the piano (some consider that it already has). The instrument offers several performance capabilities akin to those of acoustic string and wind instruments, possibilities the piano does not offer. These specialties include the use of **drawbars**, **percussive modes**, and the **Leslie** speaker cabinet, as well as the addition of various amounts of **distortion**. Through the use of these devices, a player can change and manipulate the sound of the instrument while playing, much like a string or wind player can alter the timbral qualities of a single note while holding it.

Drawbars

The drawbars subtract or add harmonics (or overtones) from/to the fundamental pitch. Simply put, a pitch produced by any instrument actually consists of additional pitches above the *fundamental* pitch (the main "note" that you hear), and these extra pitches are softer than the fundamental, yet contribute to the sound quality of the note. These additional pitches, called *overtones* or *harmonics*, and what proportion of volume they are to each other and the fundamental, are what allows your ear tell the difference between, for example, a violin and a clarinet sounding the same note. The drawbars on an organ represent harmonics that can be added to or subtracted from a fundamental pitch to produce different timbres. Pulling out drawbars adds harmonics, while pushing them in reduces them. When all drawbars are fully pulled out, the result is a rich, thick sound. Conversely, only having one drawbar pulled out produces a thin but pure sound. Not only can one experiment with different drawbar settings to get a certain sound, but the bars can be moved while playing, in real time. Gradual timbral changes, even crescendos and decrescendos can be produced with this function as well as simply changing the sound quality over time. The result, through practice and experimentation on the instrument, is a keyboard with great expressive capabilities.

The next example demonstrates the timbral changes produced by real-time adjustments of the drawbars. The track is reflective of the ending to "Carry On Wayward Son" by Kansas, which employs a gradual pushing in of the drawbars from low to high to give the impression of a "fading out" effect. The organ sound begins with all drawbars fully pulled out, and then each drawbar is pushed in, one at a time, from lowest to highest, until only the top bar is left pulled out on the last whole note.

TRACK 2

Drawbar use is not commonly notated, but you can experiment with altering the positions while playing to help in dynamic shading and other effects. The next example demonstrates the opposite of the previous one, a drawbar-created crescendo.

TRACK 3

The final drawbar example takes the same chord as in the previous two examples, and randomly manipulates the drawbars, in real-time. Listen for the great variance in timbre. No other notes are being played. This is done only with the drawbars.

TRACK 4

Percussive mode

Percussive mode adds a "click" sound to the attack of detached notes. When slurring one note to the next, the percussion will not sound, but separation of notes provides for individual articulation. Organs may offer one or more types of percussion, and digital organ simulations also offer multiple percussion settings. As with the drawbars, this setting can also be turned on and off while playing for added expression.

Below we see an example using percussive effects. Listen for the difference between the slurred notes and articulated notes (indicated with staccato markings) on the track.

TRACK 5

This percussion effect allows the player to employ phrasing much like a wind player with respect to tonguing vs. slurring, or a string player in bowing multiple notes in one stroke vs. multiple notes in separate, individual strokes.

Leslie and Vibrato

Finally we come to a very common addition to the organ, the **Leslie**, a speaker than spins inside a heavy wooden cabinet. A player can turn on and off the spinning feature, as well as adjust the speed of the spin (usually a fast and slow speed). If you don't have the real Leslie speaker, many synthesizers and digital organs include a Leslie effect, offering a simulation of the spinning speaker with various speeds.

In the next track, listen for the Leslie speaker effect while this simple C major scale is played. On the way up, beginning with the second note, the spinning speaker is turned on, then off, on every-other note. You can hear that the effect is not simply on or off, but actually hear the spinning speed up when turned on, then slow down and stop when turned off. A *tremolo* sign has been added to the notes played with the speaker in full spin.

TRACK 6

This is yet another effect that can be employed in real-time, or, you can simply have the speaker spinning or not throughout an entire song. Real organs will usually have some sort of manual switch to throw in order to change the speed, or start and stop the spinning. Some digital organs offer a motion-sensing controller: when your hand passes over a kind of electric eye, the spinning simulation of the speaker will begin; when you pass your hand over again, the spinning speaker simulation stops.

Distortion

Besides the previously mentioned effects, Hammond players can apply guitar-type distortion effects, producing that distinctive "Deep Purple" sound. The following demonstrates two different organ sounds utilizing distortion. In the first phrase (A) the distortion is relatively mild, while the lower-register second phrase (B) uses a heavy distortion. The effect of the distortion is enhanced through "power chord"-like motifs (harmonic 5ths and 4ths), similar in function to a guitar.

Such guitar-like figures can either act as a guitar substitute during a guitar solo, or can double the guitar to add extra heaviness. And like the previously mentioned effects, distortion can be employed in real-time. You can gradually turn on/up and down/off the distortion as you are playing.

Another technique commonly employed on the Hammond, but not unique to just the organ, is **glissando**, a sliding up and/or down the keyboard for special effect. This can be particularly effective in aggressive passages. See the Chapter 8 tunes, "Welcome 2 the Show" and "Solar Winds" for examples of organ glissando technique.

These are only a small fraction of the capabilities of the Hammond organ (and similar digital organs). One way to learn is to experiment with these effects through improvisation. You can also develop your technique for real-time manipulation through exercises such as scales. Instead of playing scales on a piano, practice right hand scales while the left hand manipulates the drawbars (see more on scale practice in Chapter 6). Do the same with turning on and off the spinning of the Leslie speaker, the percussion effects, and distortion. These types of exercises will get you accustomed to the full expressive real-time potential of this instrument.

In conclusion, though there are many effects available on the organ, one does not have to use all of them all of the time. It is perfectly fine to "program" a setting you like and keep it there for an entire solo or tune. Employ a balance of manipulating these effects in real-time, and just letting a certain sound be played unaltered. Experimenting with these proportions should produce interesting and never tiresome Hammond organ parts. Also, there are many digital versions of the Hammond that share the same capabilities, so you don't have to lug around the "real thing"—which can be very heavy and take up a lot of space.

Mellotron

Though used in many styles of popular music in the '60s and '70s, the **Mellotron** has come to be known as one of the most characteristic keyboard sounds in progressive rock. One of the earliest and most notable keyboard intros featured the instrument's famous flute sound in the Beatles' "Strawberry Fields." This instrument had individual three-track tapes of recorded instruments for each key on its three-octave keyboard. Pressing a key was basically like pressing "play" on a tape-recorder, which would play a recording of the specified pitch that had been recorded by "real" instruments. Each note could last for up to about eight seconds before running out of tape. The most popular sounds were string sections, flutes, brass, and voice choirs. So, for example, when one pressed "middle C" on the keyboard, a tape recording of a string orchestra playing that pitch would sound. Due to this instrument's unique capabilities (and limitations), it was—and still is—very distinctive.

The original Mellotrons were very temperamental, requiring constant maintenance and upkeep. With the advent of digital technology it became possible to sample the sounds of the original Mellotrons, and play them on modern synthesizers. However, in order to truly capture the Mellotron sound on digital instruments, a player should keep in mind the limitations of the original (some software versions of the Mellotron have these limitations built in). For example, do not hold any note for longer than eight seconds, and limit quick-response playing of a repeated note (the tape needs a bit of time to rewind). This instrument is best used for playing chords, longer-note melodies, and anything else to fill in the texture, creating a lush, symphonic sound. Using it to play quick, scalar passages and virtuosic solos should be avoided if you wish to sound authentic.

Bands such as Yes and Genesis employed the Mellotron often in their early years. More recently, groups such as Spock's Beard, the Flower Kings, and Änglagård have used the instrument to capture that '70s symphonic prog sound. Countless others have used it as well, helping the Mellotron to become one of the prominent icons in progressive rock.

The following is an example in the style of Genesis, who relied heavily upon the Mellotron in their early days. This uses the Mellotron strings/brass sound.

TRACK 8

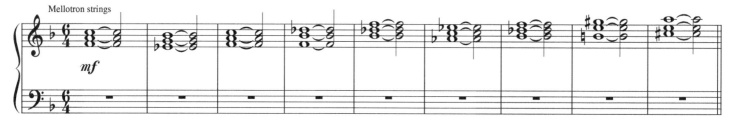

With added reverb, this sound produces a lush symphonic backdrop. While not sounding exactly like a combination of real strings and brass, the sampled instruments of the Mellotron produce a distinctive substitute. Many digital synthesizers offer either Mellotron samples, or Mellotron-like patches. If you do not have access to these sounds, try a string ensemble patch, layered with brass, and add large-hall reverb. The same will work for the choir sounds.

Several newer prog bands, many of which came into being in the 1990s, employ the Mellotron to evoke a classic '70s prog sound. To demonstrate two additional favorite sounds, flute and choir, this next example is in the style of the more recent bands Änglagård and Spock's Beard.

TRACK 9

Last but not least, our next example demonstrates one of the Mellotron string sounds, used prominently by Rick Wakeman in Yes. This is a bit different from the strings/brass sound demonstrated earlier, and offers an even more sumptuous sound for symphonic backdrop due to the lack of the brass timbre. The example does show how the sound can be used to play the melody as well, heard in the top voice of the right hand.

TRACK 10

Though in pop music the Mellotron is mainly a thing of the past, many prog bands have embraced it as a definitive progressive rock sound.

Moog/Minimoog

First introduced around 1970, the **Minimoog** is monophonic (one can only play one pitch at a time—no harmony), and is thus used mostly for melodic lines and "lead" solos. This keyboard also possessed **oscillators**, devices that cause repeating fluctuations in voltage to produce the pitch. These oscillators could drift out of tune as a result of numerous factors (stage vibration, temperature, etc.), and had to be checked often and carefully tuned. A large portion of the development of the instrument was initiated by Keith Emerson (of ELP), whose demands in live performance spawned a collaboration with the instrument's creator in order to make it more performance-friendly. (It was originally a studio instrument, not intended for live performance—especially in a rock band.)

Whereas the Mellotron is often used for lush background parts, the Minimoog sound cuts through the texture, making it great for lead solos. Many of the analog synth solos from the '70s featured this instrument, or others that were similar in style. One of the most famous Minimoog solos in progressive rock occurs near the end of ELP's popular song "Lucky Man." This next example features a solo in this style.

TRACK 11

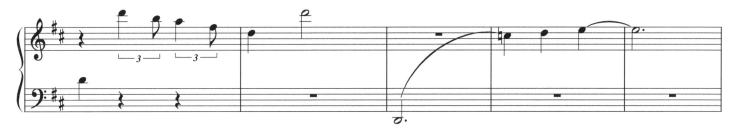

This solo (and sound) was so distinctive at the time that many digital synthesizers today have a Minimoog-like patch called "Lucky Man." So (though diehard fans would argue this), you don't really need to have the actual vintage instrument to capture the '70s prog sound of the Minimoog.

The Moog and its many synthesizer versions offer a **portamento** function which allows for a glissando between notes that are slurred. This feature can be exploited as in this last example. Allowing space between notes will provide for a clean attack, but slurring notes together will cause the instrument to slide from one to the next. Most synthesizers and software instruments allow one to program just how fast this slide will be. It can be programmed so fast as not to be noticeable at all, or slow enough to produce a siren-like effect. When playing with a sound like this, be careful to articulate each note when you do *not* want the sliding sound.

The next example is in the style of Rush, as this Canadian band often made use of Moog-based melodies in their music's quieter moments. With the melody functioning like an orchestral oboe or clarinet solo, Rush's keyboard melodies are a great example of distinctive prog keyboard soloing without the need for over-whelming virtuostic technique.

TRACK 12

These examples represent only a very small sampling of the sounds the Moog can produce. This instrument offers a variety of **timbres** (overall sound qualities: bright, dark, etc.), and can cut through loud aggressive sections, or take on a more mellow tone to be used in quieter sections such as our Rush-like example. Sounds can also be constructed that take on a percussive quality, used for rhythmic accompaniment parts. On digital synthesizers, you can alter your Minimoog patches to make them brighter or darker to serve your purpose. More examples of Minimoog (or Minimoog-like) playing are featured in Chapter 8, as well as in several other examples throughout the book.

The above four instruments represented the quintessential keyboard sound in 1970s progressive rock, where most sound sources came from pre-digital instruments. Today, in the twenty-first century, progressive rock artists often use these classic sounds to help revive that '70s spirit. When mixed with newer digital sounds and other instruments, the result can be surprisingly original, with hints of the '70s sound helping to connect the "classic" to the "contemporary."

Digital Synthesizers

In the 1980s, when progressive rock went mostly underground, digital technology exploded. Many artists wishing to modernize their sound turned to digital synthesizers, attempting to create new and original sonorities. Synthesizer patches covered a wide range, from the more percussive piano-like sounds, to lush Mellotron colors, as well as many varieties of cut-through lead-synth patches that often resembled the timbral qualities of the electric guitar.

Lead patches

Among the groups to take advantage of digital sounds were some of the progressive metal bands that began in the '80s. Keyboards often blended with and doubled lead-guitar lines, adding to the guitar sound without obscuring it. A distinctive soloing characteristic was to have quick, scalar-based solos sounding in unison with or parallel to the guitar. One of the bands to take advantage of this was Dream Theater. Considered to be one of the first progressive metal bands, with regular output from 1989 to the present, a variety of lead-synth sounds have been used by the group's three primary keyboard players over the years.

Though these digital lead patches were often used in conjunction with guitar solos, the synth could also stand on its own. Whether cutting through the thick heavy metal rhythm guitar, or soloing in a more delicate passage, digital synths were capable of a wide variety of sonorities.

This next example, in the style of Dream Theater, features a lead synth line, with a sound designed to cut through the heavy rhythm guitar texture.

TRACK 13

Note the use of pitch-bend pitches as well as vibrato. These elements will be discussed in greater detail in Chapter 6.

Background/"wash" patches

Digital synths not only provide patches for lead solo playing, but also contain many sounds for resonant symphonic backdrops, much like what the Mellotron was used for in the 1970s. In addition, digital technology offers a wealth of atmospheric sonorities, including sounds that posses long **envelopes**—sounds that change over time. The British band Ozric Tentacles often uses an extensive palette of digital synthesizer patches to help bring a certain modern spaciness to their music. The next examples span three different tracks. Each demonstrates the same part, played with different patches exhibiting a variety of long-envelope "wash" sonorities over the same groove.

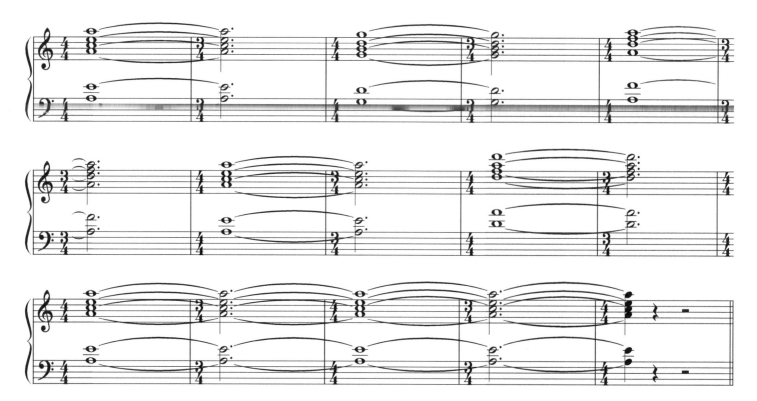

As you can tell from this example, the part is very easy to play, and it's the patch that really does all the work. This type of effect is great for a break from more virtuosic playing. It can provide a backdrop for solos, or simply stand up on its own as an atmospheric scrim.

To achieve a similar effect, find (or program) a patch with a slow attack (the sound fades in, as opposed to an accented attack) and a long release. This will enable the musical lines to blur together, providing a kind of foggy musical landscape. This style of playing will also be greatly enhanced through the use of **layered patches**.

Layering

A great way to create lush and colorful sounds on your digital keyboards is to experiment by layering multiple sounds together. Even the simplest keyboards have a layering function, with the ability to blend at least two patches together. More advanced synthesizers offer the opportunity to layer many different sounds together. A patch that may not sound particularly interesting or unique by itself can often be just the right ingredient to add to another sound, creating a much richer sonority than the individual patch. Something as simple as a blend of strings and brass can give your keyboard parts a huge symphonic sound. The next example demonstrates a symphonic prog rock section utilizing these two common and ordinary sounds blended together.

TRACK 17

The string patch by itself lacks punch, and a lot of brass synths can sound too dry and cold. Layering these two patches together hides the negative qualities and brings out the positive characteristics of each sound.

This layering function not only works for symphonic backdrops, but can also be very useful in lead solo patches. The following solo is played three times on the track: the first with a Moog-like lead patch, the second with an organ sound, and the third using both patches layered together. Playing these two sounds in unison in this manner is something that was not really achievable in the 1970s, before digital technology came into being.

Take some time and experiment with layering patches together until you find the right combinations to suit your needs. Digital synthesizers also have a multitude of programming capabilities, which means you can take a "preset" and alter various aspects of the original sound to create your own patch. Besides helping to create sounds for use in particular tunes, the above processes can help spawn musical ideas. The act of manipulating and blending patches, and then playing with them, can produce just the right creative spark, something upon which to base an entire composition.

There are many other avenues that could be explored with respect to keyboard instruments, including samplers, electric pianos, and a wide variety of additional vintage and modern instruments. However, even with something as simple as the traditional piano, you can create all kinds of interesting prog keyboard parts. Using a combination of the first four sounds/instruments listed in this chapter can help you capture that unique prog sound for playing your own songs, or tackling the tunes of the great progressive rock bands.

Chapter 3

RHYTHM AND METER

Meter

One instantly identifiable characteristic of a lot of progressive rock is changing meter and odd meter. A lot of [illegible] "groove" usually remains constant for an uninterrupted flow. In prog, however, changing meter provides an element of surprise and unpredictability, adding drama and suspense.

The following example is in the style of Kansas, one of the earliest and best known American progressive rock groups. Though the pulse is steady, with 4/4 being the predominant meter, one beat is subtracted from the fourth measure (a 3/4 bar), making the phrase structure just a touch more irregular. When the phrase repeats (measures 5–9), an extra measure is added to the end (meas. 9) of the verse to help prepare for the chorus. Finally, the last four bars show the chorus of the tune, which also takes advantage of a combination of 4/4 and 3/4 meters.

TRACK 19

Though the meter indeed changes, it still remains a **simple meter**, one with a quarter-note pulse throughout. Simple meter is also defined by the fact that this quarter-note pulse is divided into groups of two—eighth notes are the primary subdivision of the beat within the music. With the quarter-note pulse remaining constant, the changes may not necessarily be perceived by listeners, unless they attempt to count along. Still, this provides that added metrical edge to the tune, giving it a less than predictable quality.

In **compound meter**, the basic pulse is divided into three. Thus 6/8 would be a compound meter in that the pulse, being represented by the dotted quarter note, is divided into three eighth notes. An **odd meter** may be one where the pulse division is not the same for each beat. In 5/8 meter, one pulse may consist of three eighth notes, and the other, two. How each pulse is divided depends on the music. A 5/8 meter with the compound subdivision on the first beat may be referred to as "3+2." A 7/8 measure could be indicated as being "3+2+2." A 9/8 meter would be compound only if its divisions consist of "3+3+3." However, it would be considered odd if the pulse divisions were "2+2+3+2"—it all depends on the musical figure at hand, and how it is accented.

This next example is in the style of the quieter side of Dream Theater. The first phrase is in 5/8, with a "3+2" subdivision. The second four-bar phrase (measures 5–8) is similar to the first, but in 6/8—a subtle, but effective use of **repetition** and **variation**. (See Chapter 7 for more on repetition and variation.)

TRACK 20

A common method in constructing phrases in odd and changing meter is to take a more "square" phrase and add or subtract a beat. This is especially useful when material returns within a song. Rather than state the same thing twice, changing the meter in some way adds an extra quirk of unpredictability, something common in progressive rock.

Another example of mixing compound and simple meters is seen in this next excerpt in the style of Yes. A simple six-note motif utilizing only four pitches is repeated several times, with the rhythm changing slightly but noticeably, dictating this meter change. The 9/16 bars give the motif a temporary swing-like feel. Also note how the figure alternates between one measure of 9/16, and then two measures of 9/16, between each measure of 3/4.

TRACK 21

The sixteenth-note subdivision remains constant throughout the changing meters, as you will hear in the drum part on the track.

Some of the roots of the use of odd meter come from the folk music of Eastern Europe. This music frequently combines small cells made up of two, three, or four beats that form larger groups of 5/8, 7/8, 9/8, and even 10/8 measures. Twentieth-century classical composer Béla Bartók used this rhythmic folk element in many of his compositions. His works—along with the compositions of Igor Stravinsky who also employed the use of folk music and odd meters—serve as a strong influence on much progressive rock.

The following example takes on this rhythmic flair, created in the style of the Belgian RIO group Univers Zero. Two tracks (the first *slow*, the second at *full speed*) have been included to enable you to hear clearly the meter changes and timing along.

TRACK 22
slow

TRACK 23
full speed

Notice how this example is similar to the previous Yes-like example in that it takes a small figure or motive and repeats it several times. Each time it is played, it is varied slightly by adding or subtracting a few notes, yet it remains essentially the same motif. The accents are very important in bringing out the rhythmic character in the subdivisions. Also listen to how the bass and drum parts underscore these accents.

Metric modulation

This device was first notably used by twentieth-century classical composer Elliott Carter. In **metric modulation**, a tempo change occurs by making some kind of note in the first tempo equal to a different kind of note in the second tempo. This is best demonstrated in the following example. The tune begins in 6/8, with a dotted-quarter-note pulse at 112 BPM (beats per minute). In measure 5, the meter changes to 4/4, with a quarter-note pulse of 84 BPM. In this change, the eighth-note value in the 6/8 measures is temporarily equivalent to the sixteenth-note value in the 4/4 measures. Thus, when switching to 4/4, it is like accenting every four notes instead of every three.

TRACK 24

Notice how the right-hand notes don't actually change speed/duration, but how they are grouped and accented gives a feeling of a time shift. This shift is accentuated by the left hand, bass, and drum parts, as you will hear on the track.

Also note the "($♪$ = $♪$)" symbol at the change. In this musical example, this is to let the player know that the *pulse* changes tempo, (dotted quarter-note pulse becomes quarter-note pulse). Without this, one might assume that the quarter-note pulse in 4/4 retains the same tempo as the dotted-quarter pulse in the preceding 6/8—a different effect entirely, as demonstrated in the next example (*not* an example of metric modulation).

TRACK 25

In this example, the pulse remains the same, but the note values change. There is no feeling of a time shift as in metric modulation, but for the sake of notation, it is important to be able to read and write the difference. However, in progressive rock, it is this *feeling* of a time shift that we're after, that which puts some adventurousness into the music.

When performing this type of change, the notational aspect can make it seem overly complicated and mathematical. One can really just listen and feel the change. As a keyboard player performing and composing your own progressive rock tunes, experiment with this device in your playing, and don't think about the notation aspects until after you have the feel you want. Then, when it comes time to communicating the music to the rest of the group, you may either notate, demonstrate through playing and a recording, or both. This is up to you.

The next example shows how one particular motif is played exactly the same throughout, though the tempo and meter changes. This type of motif has been used by many progressive rock and even heavy metal bands throughout the years. Although the piano, guitar, and bass parts all remain the same, it is the drums that control the shift in pulse. Listen for this metric modulation on the track, then play along. This effect occurs in the music of bands like Dream Theater, whose signature style is led by "playing with time," via methods that engage and amuse the listener.

TRACK 26

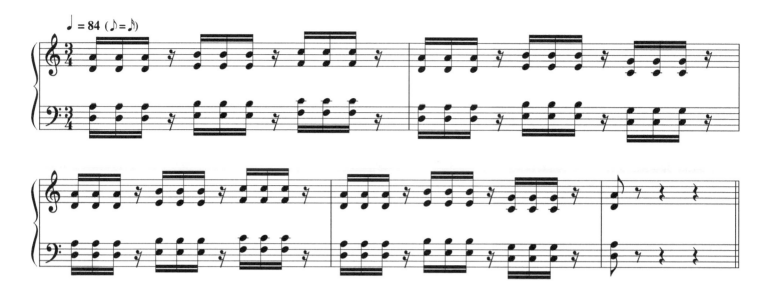

In order to pull off this kind of time shift, you must keep your part very steady to better enable the drummer to control the change in pulse. Without the drum part, one would not hear the metric modulation. Also note how the drummer continues "playing with time" in going "double time" in the final two measures. Again, you may go by the feel of this modulation, and only need to worry about the "meter math" if you'll be notating or reading this. The important thing is to establish the proper feel as you play. (The BPM in the 3/4 meter is derived by taking the 112 from the 6/8 measures and multiplying it by .75: 112 X .75 = 84).

Rhythm
Syncopation

Changing meter itself may be seen as a form of **syncopation**. The term refers to any rhythmic element that "distracts" from a steady, predictable pulse. Meter aside, syncopation also refers to rhythms in between the solid pulse of the beats. Successive attacks of notes in between the beats rather than on them is a common trait.

Example **A** below demonstrates a non-syncopated figure—it sounds pretty *square*. Example **B** takes the same figure and syncopates it by anticipating certain notes by half a beat through the use of ties. These notes end up taking on a natural accent, but the syncopation is further enhanced by fully accenting these notes, which can be greatly helped by the drums or other instruments playing the same accents.

TRACK 27

Any time you create a keyboard line, think about the potential for greater rhythmic interest through syncopation, anticipating certain beats as in the previous example.

The next example demonstrates a different type of syncopation, one where a more percussive figure is created by playing short rhythmic groupings, shifting when they begin on the beat, and when they begin off the beat. A greater syncopated effect is achieved by varying the length of these cells, making it more unpredictable.

This example is in the style of Kansas, but similar figures have been used by bands like Rush, Dream Theater, and many more. In our example, most of the band plays this syncopated figure in unison while the guitar (not notated) plays a melody over the top.

TRACK 28

This type of syncopated figure works well at climatic moments. Played softly, it can also provide an interesting introduction to a tune. When playing this, it may be useful to tap your foot on the beats in order to better feel the off-beats, and keep the syncopation tight between all players in the group.

Cross rhythms

Like changing meter and odd meter, and metric modulation, this is another device that gives the impression of time manipulation. Though the meter may remain constant, a rhythmic pattern consisting of a different length than that of the meter is repeated, thereby beginning on different beats each measure. For example, if the time signature is 4/4, a pattern that is only three beats in length, when repeated without pause, will start on beat 4 the second time, then beat 3 the third time, etc. Thus it begins in different spots "across" the measure, or extends across the bar line. If it is repeated enough, it will eventually begin back on beat one again (in this case, the fifth time the pattern is played).

Why not just make the meter 3/4, so the pattern will always begin on beat 1, and everything will be neatly in line? Well, this is progressive rock, and having everything neatly in line can be boring; prog players like to shake things up a bit, especially when it comes to issues of time. So even though our pattern is three beats long, other instruments can simultaneously play patterns that are four beats in length. It is the relationship (or conflict) between these patterns of different lengths that makes things interesting.

In this next example, the main rhythmic motif is played in the right hand. Inside 4/4 meter, this motive is only three beats long. Thus, it begins again on beat 4 of the first measure, then again on beat 3 of the second measure, beat 2 of measure three, and back to beat 1 in measure 4. The keyboard part uses the classic Minimoog sound.

TRACK 29

What makes this interesting is not necessarily the motif itself, but the context in which it is placed, including the bass and drum parts that go with it. If it weren't for the accompanying parts, this motive could simply be notated and/or felt in 3/4, and nothing would be special about it. But here the bass and drums follow the 4/4 structure, strengthening the meter, and making the three-beat pattern in the keyboards sound even more out of sync.

Next time you're called upon to create some sort of **comping** (accompaniment) part on the keys, try coming up with a pattern that is a different length than the measure. You may have to try out several patterns to find one that works. The "out of sync" feeling still has to gel with the other parts, so not all cross-rhythmic parts may work. This is fun to experiment with.

A common rhythmic technique in progressive rock is to suddenly put all the other instruments in sync with the cross-rhythmic pattern. The next example shows the same keyboard part as in the previous example, but after three bars, the meter changes to 3/4, and the other instruments play in sync with the cross-rhythmic pattern (making it no longer cross-rhythmic). Listen for this change on the track.

TRACK 30

Take advantage of moving in and out of sync with the other parts in the band. This will give your listeners a nice surprise by adding extra rhythmic complexity, a trademark component of progressive rock. You'll make your listeners think a bit, and that extra bit of thought can be truly engaging.

Ostinato figures

An **ostinato** is a melodic and rhythmic device consisting of a short pattern, repeated persistently throughout a section or entire composition. Patterns are usually most identifiable by their rhythm, but harmonic and melodic characteristics also help give them their identity. In classical music, one of the most famous ostinatos is the rhythmic pattern from "Mars, the Bringer of War" in Gustav Holst's *The Planets*. This ostinato (a pattern in 5/4 meter) lends itself well to a progressive rock adaptation which was in fact done by Emerson, Lake & Powell on their 1986 self-titled album. Greg Lake had also played an arrangement of this piece with King Crimson back in 1969.

The following demonstrates an original progressive metal-type adaptation of this famous ostinato, played by the piano in the left hand. The right hand plays the melody on the organ.

Ostinatos often serve as a rhythmic accompaniment for solos and other instrumental interplay. As far as keyboard playing is concerned, Keith Emerson often took on the dual role of playing an ostinato with the left hand while soloing with the right. The following example is in this style. To cover a lot of ground with respect to orchestration, the left hand uses a Moog/synth sound, and the right-hand solo is played with an organ sound. (For more on the use of various keyboard sounds and instruments, see Chapter 2.)

Chapter 6 goes into greater detail on this technique, including the challenges of playing such a part, and how to overcome them.

The ostinato was also an important ingredient in minimalist music, a kind of stripped-down, pattern-repetitive music that began in the 1960s as a reaction against the increasingly complex "classical" music of academia. While minimalism was considered an off-shoot of contemporary classical music, some of it had more in common with rock. A simple pattern could be repeated over and over, with little, or no change, producing a hypnotic quality. Often the rhythmic character is what gives an ostinato its distinctiveness as opposed to any melodic or harmonic properties. Several progressive rock bands made minimalism a part of their style, employing lengthy ostinatos in their music. Such groups included Magma, Univers Zero, and Present. (See Chapter 8, "Revenge of the Insects" for a complete example.)

The following example is in the style of the Belgian band Present. Though the piano part remains constant, in listening to the track you will hear how the bass and drums change around it. Also note how the minor variations in the piano help give the part at least a bit of forward motion to keep it from getting stagnant.

TRACK 33

However, just *how* an ostinato is used and varied can yield all kinds of possibilities. An ostinato can move back and forth from foreground to background, with other elements in the composition changing around this constant repetitive element. The pattern could also migrate among different instruments, keeping things fresh.

Just how you create and use ostinatos in your keyboard playing is up to you. Pay careful attention to how long your pattern repeats, as well how much and what kind of variation it undergoes. What you do with it could mean the difference between something that is engagingly hypnotic or boring and mundane.

Summary

The importance of rhythm and meter cannot be understated! All the techniques described in this chapter play a major role in defining the progressive rock style. In other types of popular music, the instrumental parts serve the vocals/lyrics by providing a grooving backdrop, one often used for dancing. In progressive rock, the manipulation of time takes the music into an adventurous world where these temporal effects engage and stimulate the listener. These techniques provide for many wonderful surprises, twists, and turns, so take great care in rhythmic and metrical considerations when creating your keyboard parts. You must also beware not to employ too many changes just for the sake of change, but give meaning and purpose to them, and connect them to other parts of the music. (See more on form, development, and musical relationships in Chapter 7.)

Chapter 4

HARMONY

Progressive rock contains a wide variety of harmonic schemes. While much rock 'n' roll is based on the I, IV, and V chords of a given key (and other progressions based on a strong dominant-tonic relationship), progressive rock often expands well beyond these progressions, offering alternatives to dominant-tonic harmonic structures. Some prog mimics jazz harmony, utilizing **extended chords**, and **chromaticism** (using chords outside of the key, as well as frequent key changes). Progressive rock tunes can also follow a **late-Romantic** type of harmony (i.e., Wagner), early-twentieth-century **Impressionist** sonorities (i.e., Debussy), or **atonal** harmonic schemes (i.e., Stravinsky and Bartók). Much progressive rock utilizes combinations of all of the above. For the sake of this book, we will look at a few well-known prog tunes, ones that represent the different harmonic schemes mentioned above.

Harmony Defined

The following is a brief overview of harmony basics. For more detailed instruction on harmony, please consult a music theory text book such as Mark Harrison's *Contemporary Music Theory,* Levels 1–3 (Hal Leonard Corporation).

Harmony deals with the relationship of multiple pitches sounded at the same time. A **chord** consists of any three or more pitches. Chords consisting of pitches organized or "stacked" in thirds (i.e., C, E, G, B, D) are referred to as **tertian** harmonies. A chord consisting of only the first three in the stack is called a **triad**. Triads are the basis for most tonal music (music based on the major-minor system, governed by a special relationship between the tonic and dominant). These chords consist of three parts: a **root**, **third**, and **fifth**.

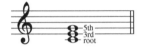

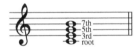

Adding a fourth note to the top of the triad (the seventh) turns the chord into a seventh chord, a type of **extended triad**.

Extensions can occur all the way up to the thirteenth as seen to the right.

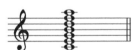

Classical composers such as Claude Debussy and Maurice Ravel utilized many extended triads in their music. In jazz, it is standard for a player, reading a chord chart or lead sheet, to add extensions to the chords as he/she sees/hears fit. Extensions add extra flavor, and can also be used to produce tension, demanding resolution.

Chord Progressions—Traditional Harmony

A **progression** is, in part, a series of chords. However, it is more than just a series. The term implies some sort of motion, and to produce motion, the relationship between chords in a series is important. Motion is created by tension and release, or conflict and resolution. Blues-based music (rock 'n' roll) often revolves around three chords: the **tonic** (I), **subdominant** (IV), and **dominant** (V). (The Roman numerals come from the note in the scale upon which each chord is based, or the chord's root. For example, in a C major scale, the first, fourth, and fifth notes are C, F, and G. Thus chords based upon these notes produce the three primary chords.)

I(C)   IV(F)   V(G)   I(C)

The C chord is our tonic chord and functions as the "home base." One may refer to the tonic as the captain of the ship (think of your favorite science fiction TV show). This is the most stable chord, and everything revolves around it. The dominant chord is the first officer. Though very important, the dominant brings everything back to the tonic. Often, the subdominant will precede the dominant as if functioning as a second officer, bringing important matters to the first officer, who then goes to the captain. Other chords in the key (II, III, VI, and VII) are of lesser rank, and therefore unstable. Like in any military situation, certain lesser-ranked members of the crew are occasionally given important responsibilities, and have to make some big decisions. However, they usually bring their ideas to the first officer, who then brings these items to the captain. Because the first officer has to deal with the rest of the crew, and at times seems more important than even the captain, the dominant chord is often given an extra pitch, the seventh. Adding the seventh to the V chord produces a special dissonance between the chord's third and seventh. This dissonant interval, known as the tritone, provides extra tension, pulling it even more strongly back to the I chord.

TRACK 34

tritone-only resolution

This system of hierarchy is the basis for most tonal music, including much blues, rock, and pop. When matters get less clear, chord progressions no longer follow this hierarchy as strictly. Things like mutiny can happen. Officers can be insubordinate, attempting to take on duties only the captain should. Outside forces come into play such as non-military individuals (aliens) visiting the ship, interacting with the crew. These may be thought of as chords outside of the diatonic scale: **chromaticism**. In the key of C major, an F♯ chord can seem very out of place. It is then up to the composer to make it work somehow. "Outside" chords need to be made relevant.

The point to all this is that the I-IV-V system has a kind of built-in organization, one that has worked for several hundred years. It is easily followed. When one wishes to delve beyond this harmonic structure, there still needs to be something in the relationship between chords, not only from one chord to the next, but among chords widely separated in time.

Extended Triads

Largely part of the jazz idiom, **extended triads** result from stacking additional thirds on top of basic triads. These extensions add tension and color to a chord without taking away its basic function. After the basic triad, extensions include the seventh, ninth, eleventh, and thirteenth. The quality (major, minor, augmented, diminished) of the chord is still determined by its basic triad, even if the extensions are altered. For example, below we see several extensions of the C major triad, beginning with the C dominant seventh (C7) up to a C13 chord with alterations.

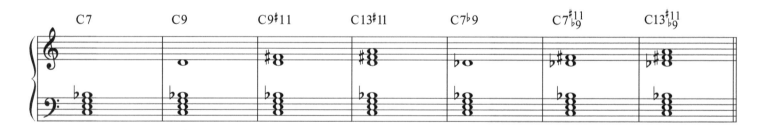

Notice that the basic C7 chord is always present.

In jazz, players often add extensions to most chords automatically, based on their ear and what level of tension they wish to produce (as well as a lot of experience in playing/improvising in the jazz idiom). What chord precedes a chord and what follows also plays an important role. A standard I–IV–V progression can be given some extra bite through the use of extensions.

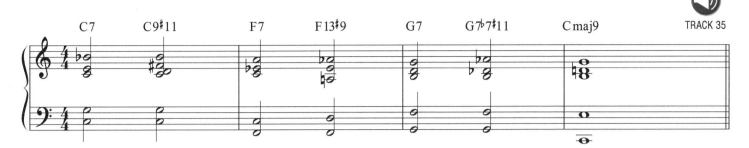

Beyond adding spice to otherwise standard progressions, extensions can help in non-standard chord progressions by producing additional **leading tones** (pitches that are led by half step to other pitches). This allows for chords to lead or pull to other chords, beyond where they would normally lead in traditional tonal music. Thus, where a particular chord is going may determine what kinds of extensions and alterations are used.

For example, the C7♭9♯11 chord contains the basic C7 chord, and a dominant chord wants to resolve to its respective tonic, which in this case would be an F triad. However, the additions of F♯ and D♭ provide potential leading tones that also want to resolve upwards to G and D; thus a G chord could follow this extended C chord, and still sound "logical."

The following shows a non-standard chord progression (beyond I–IV–V and similar progressions) that is helped in its continuity by providing leading tones through extensions and alterations. This produces tension and promotes a sense of motion.

TRACK 36

Use your ears to guide you in creating these types of chord progressions. Simply resolving a couple chord tones by a half step may not always produce the sound you want. However, you can use this half-step idea in combination with your ears to find a progression that works best for you.

Most of the time, you probably won't be called upon to create a chord progression out of nothing, but rather will be asked to provide harmony to an existing melody. Here is where the fun begins. Ordinary **diatonic** (using only pitches that belong to one key or scale) melodies can be turned into something adventurous through a more chromatic accompaniment. One may think of the melody as a character in a story, and the accompaniment as the setting. Progressive rock often puts its "characters" in fantastical settings.

The next example takes a diatonic melody in the key of C minor and harmonizes it in two different ways. Example **A** shows a simple progression using diatonic chords with few extensions. Example **B** harmonizes the melody with extended and altered chords, providing for a more colorful setting to back up the melody. **Track 37** plays examples A and B on piano along with a guitar melody. **Track 38** plays both examples, adding drums and strings (the latter doubling the piano) to put the example in a style similar to the music of Yes.

Chromaticism

The **chromatic scale** consists of all twelve pitches of our modern tuning system. In tonal music, we use a **diatonic scale** (major/minor) that contains seven pitches following a particular order of half and whole steps, and this helps determine the key. When a piece of music uses pitches and chords that do not naturally belong to that key, it is said to be **chromatic**. Such music can consist of simple major and minor triads and seventh chords, yet it will seem to change keys often, or employ chords that do not "belong" to the key.

Real music rarely stays in one key all the time without any chromatic pitches or harmonies. A mostly diatonic-sounding piece can either change key from time to time, or stay in the same key, yet introduce chromatic notes for special effects or particular functions. Progressive rock, in an attempt to get away from the blues-based I–IV–V (and other standard progressions), will often employ such chromatic harmonies, giving a tune a more colorful and adventurous quality.

One common type of chromatic harmony involves the use of **chromatic mediants**: one chord going to a chord a third away (up or down) that is not part of its implied tonality. For example, in A minor, the mediant chord would be a C major triad. One possible chromatic mediant chord would be a C triad other than major (minor, augmented, diminished)—these "altered" triads do not belong to the key of A minor. Another chromatic mediant would be a C♯ chord of any quality. Mediants also include the submediant or sixth scale degree (a third below the tonic). In our A minor example, F would be the submediant scale degree, with an F major triad functioning as the diatonic mediant. Chromatic mediant chords include F triads other than major in quality, and F♯ triads of any quality.

The first example in this section is in the space rock style of groups like Pink Floyd, Tangerine Dream, and Ozric Tentacles. Simple use of chromatic mediants helps give the music an air of mystery, promoting a suspenseful atmosphere. In C minor, the tonic chord C (with an added major 7th) starts us off. Diatonic mediants would be an E♭ major chord and an A♭ major chord. What follows is an A♭ minor chord, a chromatic mediant. After a return to the Cm(maj7), comes an E minor triad. The track uses an especially eerie-sounding patch to aid in the suspense already created by the chromatic mediants.

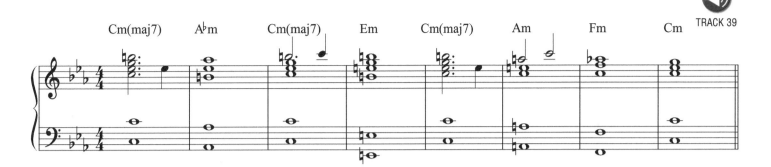

With the space rock sub-genre promoting hallucinogenic imagery, this type of chromaticism is well suited for the style. If one thinks of remaining strictly in a key as being "realistic," then foray outside of that key may represent the unrealistic or fantastical. This comparison is relevant not only to psychedelic music, but to all types of prog, which often have a correlation to science fiction and fantasy, elements that transcend our natural world.

The next example is in the style of '70s Yes, exhibiting another type of subtle chromaticism, one less psychedelic. Though the tune seems to begin in E major, *none* of the other chords belong to that key. Perhaps, since the first chord is an E9, it is functioning as a dominant, and thus the tune is in A minor (the key signature indicates this). This would make more sense since all the chords other than the B♭ have a function in A minor. However, the A minor chord itself is only briefly stated in measure 6, leaving the A minor hypothesis in some doubt. Whatever the key, the progression is colorful and chromatic, without sounding too disjointed or abrupt. Each chord has something in common with, or some sort of tonal relationship to, the chord that precedes it, and the chord that follows it. For example, the opening E9 shares B and F♯ with the following B minor chord. The B minor chord shares D and B with the G chord. G is the dominant of C, and so it moves to a C chord. C and E minor share two pitches, etc. Though all chords do not seem to relate to a single key, they do progress smoothly from one to another, exhibiting either a subtle shifting of keys, or tonal ambiguity. The most drastic chromatic move is at the end, where a B♭ chord goes directly back to an E9 to begin the phrase again.

In creating such a chord progression, be careful not to go "too far" or for too long. Extended ambiguity can lose cohesion. After a while, return to the beginning and repeat the progression. Such repetition will help solidify your structure.

Late Romanticism and Impressionist Harmony

In a desire to progress beyond traditional tonal or blues-based harmony, some progressive rock adapted an impressionistic approach. One of the key impressionist composers in classical music was Claude Debussy. Whereas traditional tonal music is based upon the dominant-tonic relationship, Debussy's harmony was less about the structural relationship of chords, and more about chords as individual sonorities, and the moods created by each chord sounded one after another. In the previous section, we learned of a kind of chromaticism where each chord smoothly leads to the next, yet the whole does not remain in one clear key. With impressionistic harmony, a "smooth" change in chords was seldom cultivated. Instead, a composer such as Debussy was after various effects produced by going from one chord to the next, whether they have a tonal relationship or not. In some cases, a very "non-smooth" effect was desired. The element of surprise, mystery, or other atmospheric effect was desired.

We have learned of the tritone dissonance created in the dominant seventh chord, and that this dissonance demands a particular resolution in tonality. However, in Debussy's case, a dominant seventh chord could be followed by any other chord that produced the desired mood and effect. Following this design, one could simply experiment with playing several chords until the desired sound was achieved, not worrying about remaining in a key, or producing a progression that would "point" to a particular home base. In a sense, this style of harmony minimized the expectation of resolution.

Such a method of harmony may seem random, unorganized, and chaotic. Thus it is up to the composer/ player to find some method of unifying a group of chords to give the music direction. One method is to employ **parallel chordal movement**, choosing to utilize several chords of the same quality. To demonstrate this, we will take the dominant seventh chord. In the following, several dominant seventh chords have been chosen to make up a harmonic progression. One unifying factor is that they are all the same chord type. Another is that from one chord to the next, at least one chord tone remains in common. Use this formula in combination with your ears to produce progressions that serve your needs.

Adding rhythmic interest to the chords produces the following:

Most composers probably wouldn't often come up with the chord sequence and the rhythm as two separate processes, but would create these two elements simultaneously, perhaps to accompany a given melody. However, sometimes coming up with an interesting chord progression can help generate a melody after-the-fact. The next example adds a melody to our chord progression, as well as a bass line, created in counterpoint to the melody. (See Chapter 5 for more on counterpoint.)

TRACK 41

In listening to the example, one can hear the colorful, mood-inducing nature of this harmonic method. In structuring a composition as a whole, one would then use repetition and variation of this creation to help produce meaningful music, using these concepts to build relationships, in part compensating for the lack of a traditional dominant-tonic relationship.

The next example featuring parallel chord movement is in the style of Yes, using the Mellotron strings sound. The progression uses a series of major ninth chords, with only the first harmony being diatonic (belonging to the key).

TRACK 42

Notice the moody effect achieved by these extended harmonies, one after another, with no move toward a tonic or dominant. Impressionistic ideals also see a direct parallel in some of the lyrics of Yes, whose meaning is not always clear as a whole, but consist of words and phrases put together to create certain imagery and moods, much akin to the goals of impressionistic harmony.

Finally, for a darker, more mysterious mood, one could try another type of parallel chord movement, using successive minor chords, and *only* minor chords. In tonality, a major key consists of three major triads (I, IV, V), three minor triads (ii, iii, iv), and one diminished triad (vii°). This combination of chords sets up a nice system of tension and release, promoting movement between the "happy" and "sad" chords. By employing only minor chords, the effect is a bit jarring and darker.

One group known for employing this tactic was Sweden's Änglagård, a symphonic progressive band from the early 1990s, who played instrumental music in a classic '70s prog style. The next example is in the style of this group's sometimes dark music, utilizing only minor chords.

TRACK 43

The tonal center of the piece is D, as indicated by the D minor key signature. The roots of all the chords are diatonic to the key of D minor, but the qualities of all the chords are not. If the piece were diatonically in D minor, the C and B♭ chords would be major, and the E chord would be diminished. Changing these chords to minor removes their tonal function, and produces something quite different. Though the harmonies are darker and less tonal in function, the repetition element of "all minor chords" is a unifying factor in the composition.

Atonality

This section will feature common sources of pitch material other than the major-minor tonal system, focusing on scales and collections.

Much of the music in progressive rock takes on characteristics of classical music from before 1900. Music from the Baroque, Classical, and Romantic periods was tonal; that is, it was based largely on the major-minor system, utilizing corresponding scales and triads, as well as following harmonic progressions designed to revolve around a "home base" or tonic. The twentieth century saw an abandonment of the tonal system by many composers, most notably Arnold Schoenberg, Anton Webern, Alban Berg, Igor Stravinsky, and Béla Bartók to name a few. These composers adopted systems of pitch and harmony that were not based in tonality: **atonal** music.

Synthetic scales

There are many scales beyond the major, minor, and traditional modes, with a variety of colorful names attached. The following shows a few of the most common used by some of the great twentieth-century classical composers as well as progressive rock bands in the RIO sub-genre. Though this chapter is devoted to harmony, the following synthetic scales are also applied to melody. As a keyboard player, if you wish to utilize these scales in your playing and composing, it is highly recommended that you practice them as part of your daily warm up. Fingerings have been included in the following examples, but multiple fingerings are possible. Feel free to come up with your own.

The **whole tone scale** is simple—six pitches, each a whole step apart, and only two scales are possible. Starting on C, the pitches are C, D, E, F♯, G♯, A♯. Starting on C♯, we get C♯, D♯, F, G, A, B. If we begin on any other pitch, we end up with one of the two collections mentioned above. What makes this scale unique is its lack of half steps. Without this interval, the music can seem to float, making it a challenge to promote tension and release.

whole-tone scales

Harmonic possibilities include the augmented triad and the dominant seventh chord (minus the fifth, which is commonly omitted). Non-tonal chords include anything else using the six pitches. In composing a keyboard part, one can create progressions from the scale and repeat them.

The following shows a chord progression created from the whole tone scale in the left hand, along with a melody in the right. In measure 5, the music switches to the "other" whole tone scale, following the same progression, with the melody continuing in a phrase that responds to the first four measures. The very last measure returns to the first whole tone scale to help provide finality.

TRACK 44

The lack of half steps in this pitch collection can produce music with an un-grounded quality. Half steps often lead to other harmonies and help resolve tension. Without leading tones, the music can seem to wander, so use this pitch system carefully, for appropriate effect and mood.

The **octatonic scale** (or diminished scale, as it is commonly referred to in jazz) utilizes another symmetrical pattern, a regular alternation of whole and half steps. With this arrangement, there are only three possible collections of pitches.

half-whole starting on C   whole-half starting on C   whole-half starting on B

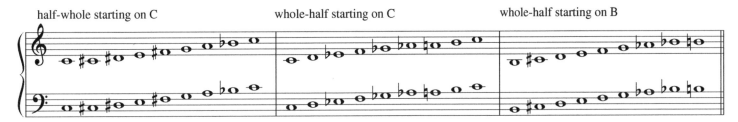

The scale can either begin with the half step, or the whole step. If you begin on C with a whole step, you get one scale; beginning on C with a half step results in another scale. There is only one scale left—begin on B with a whole step. Starting on any other pitches, with either whole step first or half step first will result in one of the three scales/collections already mentioned.

The makeup of this scale results in more tritones and half steps than in the major or minor scales. This produces the possibility for extra dissonance, which can facilitate dark-sounding music, as is heard in quite a few of the RIO bands. Major and minor triads can also be drawn from this scale. Depending on how one uses the scale, music based on it can sound quite consonant, and almost tonal, especially when tertian structures are derived from it.

The next example shows one octatonic scale and all major and minor chords that can come out of it. Each chord is also extended, showing its seventh.

So if you want to get some "familiar" sound out of this scale, there are many options for tertian chords. However, there is no dominant-tonic relationship. For example, above we saw a C chord, but its dominant, G, cannot be constructed from the scale. Without this dominant-tonic relationship, you are forced to pull away from traditional tonal tendencies when using this scale strictly.

Finally, we'll put these characteristics into a musical setting. Throughout the next example, the left hand plays chords while the right hand plays a melody. The first four measures see a more consonant harmony using traditional chords derived from the octatonic scale (thus these chords are labeled). The music turns darker in the middle as the harmony becomes more dissonant (measures 5–8). The last four bars see a melding of the consonant and dissonant styles as if the first section returns, but tainted by elements from the darker middle section. All of the music is taken from the pitches of the C half-whole octatonic scale.

TRACK 45

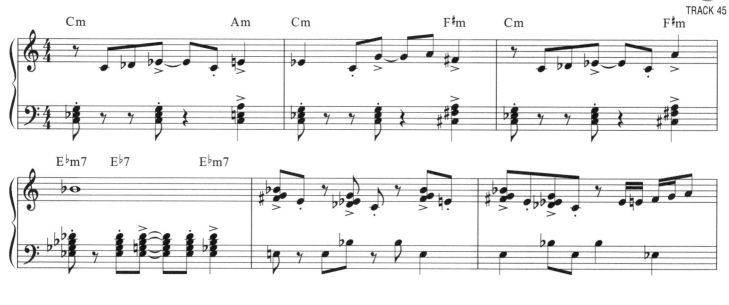

The previous example takes on the style of RIO bands such as Univers Zero and Present, who use synthetic scales, much like Stravinsky and Bartók, to create dark and dissonant rock music. (See "Revenge of the Insects" in Chapter 8, for a full RIO-styled tune utilizing the octatonic scale.)

The **hexatonic** scale uses the pattern of minor second–minor third in alternation to form a six-note collection.

C hexatonic

Much like the whole tone scale, this collection can be limiting, due to the fewer number of pitches involved. It does however fill in a gap in that it is the opposite of the whole tone scale (there are no major seconds). In alternation with the whole tone scale, these two collections can complement each other providing for contrast between musical sections.

In the following example, notice the alternating use of the hexatonic and whole tone scales. To help unify the music, both sections are based on C as a center. Also note the use of the C augmented triad which can be derived from either scale. How many other chords do the two scales have in common?

TRACK 46

For many other scales, please see *Jazzology* by Robert Rawlins and Nor Eddine Bahha (Hal Leonard Corporation), or in the "classical" realm, Vincent Persichetti's *Twentieth-Century Harmony: Creative Aspects and Practice* (W.W. Norton, 1961), a source of many aspects of post-tonal music.

Summary

When utilizing alternate pitch schemes such as synthetic scales, it is important to remember that all the hierarchical characteristics of the tonal system (dominant-tonic relationship, etc.) that can help keep the music unified and meaningful are not inherently present in the alternate pitch systems. It is therefore very important to carefully employ repetition and variation, and other musical devices to help the music "work" as a whole, giving it meaning and a sense of going somewhere.

Chapter 5
COUNTERPOINT

Harmony vs. Melody

One of the most important characteristics of progressive rock that separates it from other rock music is its use of classical music concepts. Among the most significant of these are **form** and **counterpoint**. What makes them so defining is their contrast and even opposition to how these two elements are used (or not used) in the blues-based music we know as rock 'n' roll. A standard in blues music is the twelve-bar blues form. Not only is this formally different from much classical music, but part of what makes this form identifiable is its chord-based nature. Revolving around three chords (I, IV, and V, with some variation), these chords are a major defining part of the form itself. Melodies and improvised solos are created based on this pre-existing chord progression. Though classical music can and does follow I-IV-V progressions (which pre-date blues), these progressions are more often the result of the convergence of multiple musical lines. Thus, much classical music may be thought of as more "linear based." Creating a melody, and then a bass line, and then another countermelody or two in between, produces the harmony within a tune. When looking at key points in time along these lines, such as the downbeat of each measure, and the beginning and ending of the phrase, one may see familiar chords, and familiar progressions. In fact, the essence of these convergences of lines often produced the I-IV-V progression. Blues took this essence, stripped it down, and used it as an overt structural foundation. With respect to the originality of blues, the genre did take the I-IV-V and turn them all into dominant seventh chords, sonorities that, in classical music, would demand certain resolutions; but in blues, these stood alone, unresolved—a unique characteristic.

The key difference in much classical music is that the lines came first, and the harmony resulted.

As a progressive rock keyboardist, recognizing counterpoint and its characteristics can go a long way in practicing tunes, whether by ear or reading music. If you wish to compose progressive rock, whether for just the keys or the whole band, an understanding of contrapuntal concepts is essential for capturing the style, not only on the surface, but at deeper levels of musical structure.

What is Counterpoint?

In its most simple definition, **counterpoint** means "note against note." Instead of voicing simple chords to accompany your melodies, you can create interesting countermelodies, playing two (or more) different musical lines at the same time. The practice of contrapuntal writing adds an extra complexity to the music, giving the listener a more engaging experience. Whereas rock 'n' roll may offer lots of pounding and strumming accompaniments, progressive rock tunes are often enriched by more colorful and intricate methods of adding to or backing up a melody (though pounding and strumming still certainly have their place). As a keyboard player, you can thicken up your arrangements by creating interesting lines with your left hand—all it takes is a little time and practice.

There are entire books dedicated to the study of counterpoint, but here we will examine its basics, and how it relates to progressive rock. This concept deals with the combination of two or more melodic lines, and the linear considerations that go with them. These considerations have to do with what makes two (or more) melodies sound "good" together and how, as a keyboard player, you can play these sometimes complex parts with accuracy and musicality.

Though in music history counterpoint is most associated with the Baroque period (seventeenth and early-eighteenth centuries), it is actually present in all music, from all times. A simple example of counterpoint may be a vocal melody played together with the bass. Another common form of counterpoint is "imitation" as seen in a fugue. In a **fugue**, a single melody is stated, and constantly re-stated with variation and development. This melody is then echoed in other parts, producing an "out of sync" quality. The imitation may begin a beat later than the original, or two measures later—it is up to the composer. Though the imitation can be literal (exactly the same as the original melody), it is often varied to produce a more satisfactory relationship with the original line. Keith Emerson of ELP often created fugal keyboard parts as in the introduction to the group's famous tune "Karn Evil 9."

But before we get into the prog tunes, we'll examine some of the roots of contrapuntal composition. The following example is taken from J.S. Bach's "Invention No. 1." Compare the right hand with the left. Notice how the left hand imitates the right hand, two beats later. Also look for the places where the imitation line diverts from the original.

Two-Part Invention No. 1 in C Major

TRACK 47

Johann Sebastian Bach

The first **subject** (melody) begins in the right hand, and then two beats later, as it continues, the left hand enters in imitation, resulting in two of the same basic melodies, sounded half a measure out of sync with each other. In measure 7, the left hand starts the fugue with the right hand following in imitation.

Besides understanding the concept behind this two-voice imitative counterpoint, being able to play a piece like this can prove very useful in progressive rock. The playing aspect will be looked at more closely in Chapter 6.

Whether you're playing/composing contrapuntal music in a fugal style, or simply wish to play or create two separate and distinct lines that sound good together, the key factor here is in the statement "sound good together." The imitative line may be altered from the original so it sounds good with the original line, a melody that is actually a measure or two ahead of its imitation, and thus sounding different pitches at the same time. So, what is meant by "sounds good?" First off, you can simply use your ears to determine if the two melodic lines are producing the sound you want. But in creating a countermelody, you need to make lots of choices along the way in terms of which pitches to play, and when. This can be a slow process, but there are some basic "rules" to consider that may help speed things up. Whether you use a "system" or not, the real test will always be listening to it—if it sounds good to you, it's right!

Several factors should be considered in creating "good" sounding counter lines:

Harmonic Intervals (consonance and dissonance)

Contour/Motion

Rhythm

Harmonic Intervals

A harmonic interval is the distance between two pitches played at the same time. An interval may be described by its **arithmetic distance** (2nd, 3rd, 4th, etc.) and its **quality** (major, minor, perfect, augmented, diminished). For now, we will only concern ourselves with the arithmetic distance. To figure out an interval, simply count from one letter name to the next, up or down. A *up* to C would be a 3rd: A (1), B (2), C (3) = 3rd. A *down* to C would be a 6th: A (1), G (2), F (3), E (4), D (5), C (6) = 6th. For greater detail on intervals, please consult a music theory text such as *Contemporary Music Theory*, Levels 1-3 by Mark Harrison (Hal Leonard Corporation).

When dealing with two pitches such as A and C, we call the intervals going from A up to C (3rd) and the interval going down from A to C (6th) **inversions** of each other. Thus, intervals that are inversions of each other are said to have a similar sound quality. A up to E is a 5th; A down to E is a 4th, thus 4ths and 5ths are inversions of each other.

With respect to counterpoint, the predominant interval will be 3rds and 6ths. These intervals are considered **consonant**, meaning they are stable and do not demand resolution. However, the intervals of the 5th, unison, and octave sound hollow and pure, and thus even more at rest, appropriate for finality (the end of a section or entire tune). We call these intervals **perfect consonances**, while the 3rds/6ths are referred to as **imperfect consonances**. Other intervals, such as 2nds and 7ths are considered **dissonant**—they are unstable and demand resolution. This demand for resolution creates motion within the music, a kind of "tension and release" function.

The interval of a 4th is unique in that it can be consonant or dissonant, depending on how it is sounded. When a 4th is reinforced by an additional pitch a 5th below its lowest pitch, this lower pitch helps stabilize the 4th, making it consonant. In the first example below, the 4th between the G and the C above it is considered consonant because of the lowest C, a 5th below G. When the 4th has no other pitches underneath it (as in the second example), the interval becomes unstable, thus dissonant, demanding either a resolution to a new interval, or an addition of another note below for stability.

The following excerpt has been adapted from J.S. Bach's "Invention No. 13 in A Minor." On the top staff is the main melody. Underneath is the countermelody. Notice the intervals at some of the main points (usually on each beat) between the two lines.

Two-Part Invention No. 13 in A Minor

Based on Johann Sebastian Bach

* diminished 5th

What we see is a predominance of 3rds and 6ths, with an occasional 5th and octave and one 4th. At the end of the first phrase (second measure, beat 3) we see a 5th—actually, two 5ths in a row (including the "and" of 2). The next phrase also ends with a 5th. If you remember, the 5th is hollow and open, and good for ending phrases. Notice the harmonic interval on beat 1 of the third measure. This is a 5th arithmetically speaking, but not a "perfect 5th." In order to be perfect, the distance of the 5th must be seven half-steps (based on the distance from the first to the fifth degree in the major scale). This fifth is only six half steps, and thus dissonant. Since this 5th is smaller than a perfect fifth, we call this a **diminished 5th**. This interval, and its inversion (the augmented 4th) is known as a **tritone**. In classical music from before the twentieth-century, this was considered very unstable; yet it is one of the most common dissonances, providing for the resolution from the dominant seventh chord (V7) to the tonic chord (I).

To recap, the 3rds and 6ths keep things moving by their imperfect consonant character, and make up the bulk of the music generally considered to be a pleasing sound. The perfect 5ths and octaves are used sparingly, as if the music is occasionally breathing in a momentary state of rest. Two perfect 5ths in a row solidify an ending to a phrase. The intervals of the 4th and the tritone are only used once—dissonances that help add extra tension.

Contour/Motion

There is more to creating a countermelody than simply setting up a series of harmonic intervals that seem to work well with the main melody. A **countermelody** should serve a supporting role, enabling the main melody to stand out, yet still provide some interest on its own. In order to achieve this, its own contour or shape is important. The shape of one musical line as it relates to another line being played at the same time is known as its **motion**. For example, if the main melody is moving up and the countermelody down, this is referred to as **contrary motion**. When both lines are moving the same direction (but not by the same distance), this is called **similar motion**. If they move the same direction and distance, the term **parallel motion** is applied. And finally, when one line stays the same (through repeated or held notes) while the other moves up or down, we call this **oblique motion**.

What does all this mean? Creating a countermelody can involve a lot of trial and error. Use your ears to dictate what you create, but when you get stuck, or are unsatisfied, go back to the theoretical concepts and rules to give you more options. For example, an abundance of contrary motion is usually desired to complement the main melody. (Traditional counterpoint has certain "rules," such as: a perfect interval should be approached in contrary motion.) So, when you're listening to your two melodies together, and it still does not sound quite right, check to see if contrary motion is predominant. If you have any perfect intervals (such as at the end of a phrase), look to see if they are approached in contrary motion. Something as simple as that can make a big difference in enabling your two melodies to work together and sound the way you want them to. Parallel motion should be used sparingly and briefly, for effect. This produces a distinctive sound, so a section of music with all parallel lines will stand out. This is okay as it helps give an identifying signature to the sound. However, if the whole piece, or every tune you play, is made up of mostly parallel lines, it not only loses its special effect, but can become dull and boring (think of an explosion in a movie: one or two big blasts can be very effective, but big explosions happening regularly throughout the film… you get the idea). If you take a melody and put a complete parallel line along with it, the second line is more of a coloring of the original melody rather than a countermelody.

The following examples show a melody in the right hand with a second line in the left. Example **A** adds a completely parallel line to the right-hand melody, whereas Example **B** complements the line with an independent countermelody.

TRACK 49

Example **A** is the most obvious way of adding to the melody, something common in a lot of pop and rock music. You can hear how Example B brings an extra dimension and complexity to the melody. However, both methods have their usefulness. An interesting method of composition may be to add a parallel line to a melody early in a tune, and then when the melody comes back later, accompany it with the countermelody. This can help a tune grow and develop.

In examining Example **B** a bit further, we see a predominance of contrary motion. The end of the phrase sees a perfect 5th between the two lines, which is approached by contrary motion, following the rules of traditional counterpoint. There is also at least some parallel motion, as well as oblique motion, used when the main melody holds a longer note, giving the countermelody a chance to fill in the space and keep things moving. This brings us to the third factor in creating good counterpoint: rhythm.

Rhythm

In the previous examples, besides a variance of motion, one thing that stands out is the difference in rhythm between the two lines. The rhythms coincide at points of syncopation such as the "and" of beat 2 in each measure. This helps accent these areas, bringing out the syncopation. In other places, the countermelody is more rhythmically active when the main melody is more restful. You must also consider the rhythm of a countermelody as an independent item: how does the line sound by itself, without the main melody? If you create a countermelody that can also stand alone, you have the option of using it as a main melody in other places in the tune. (You never know: sometimes, creating a countermelody leads to a new melody you find more interesting than the original. Great things can happen by accident.)

Besides creating an interesting left-hand part to go along with a right-hand melody, you can also use counterpoint to create your own lines to go along with what the guitar (or any other instrument) in your band is playing. This can help give you your own independent parts to play while still supporting another instrument that may be playing the main melody. Counterpoint can also involve more than just two melodic lines, getting into three, four, or more different lines played at the same time. As a keyboard player, you have the option of adding to the sophistication of a tune by playing one line with one sound such as organ, and another line on the piano. Meanwhile, the guitar, bass, and violin might all play their own independent melodies. Groups like Gentle Giant and Kansas often made great use of dense counterpoint involving multiple instruments.

The following example is in the style of Kansas. The piano begins the contrapuntal section with the left hand, and then the right hand enters with a countermelody on the organ. After that, other lines enter, one at a time, in the guitar and strings.

TRACK 50

This style of dense counterpoint is very overt, meaning that the counterpoint is employed not merely to give an interesting backdrop to a melody. Rather, the counterpoint itself is on display, right on the surface, and is meant to sound complicated and sophisticated.

As mentioned earlier, you don't always have to attempt to create and play two melodic lines all by yourself. Sometimes, you can focus on creating just one line to go along with a line another instrument is playing. The following example is in the style of Gentle Giant. Example **A** shows the guitar line begin, then the organ enters with a countermelody in fugal-style imitation. Example **B** shows the same guitar melody repeat itself after four measures, and an organ line that is nonimitative.

As you can see from these two examples, there are many possibilities when it comes to creating counter lines. The more different the lines are from each other, the more complex it can sound. In your progressive rock keyboard parts, determine exactly how busy a sound you want, and write your counter lines accordingly. Too much dense counterpoint all the time can become tiresome, so learn to balance this technique with simpler accompanying parts such as chords and parallel lines. A thoughtful proportion of these styles within a tune can help give the music shape, direction, growth, and variety.

Counterpoint takes time and patience, both in the creation of contrapuntal lines, and in the time you may spend practicing them. However, the extra effort is worth it, and can go a long way in helping you create progressive rock keyboard parts, those that take on some of the classical music stylings that make the genre so appealing.

Chapter 6

CHOPS

Chops refers to one's total mastery of the instrument—in other words, great technical skill in playing. Displays of virtuosity are often a part of progressive rock, on all instruments. Players must also be careful when wielding their considerable chops, for such exhibitions can overwhelm the music, making it more of a "gimmick." Chops should always serve the composition, and not the other way around. Temper and refine your keyboard parts with thoughtful consideration to solid structure, and the other compositional devices discussed in this book to give your music deep meaning. Highly developed technique is sometimes necessary in order to execute compositional ideas, but it can also provide a kind of "frosting" on the music, with displays of virtuosity adding an element of showmanship and flourish. With that being said, it is not necessary to be a complete virtuoso in order to play progressive rock. With regular practice of the following technical exercises, one can execute impressive sounding keyboard parts without having to be the next Liszt or Van Cliburn. As you will find out in this chapter, there are many things a player can execute that *sound* impressive and difficult, but are actually quite easy.

Scales

Scales represent one of the building blocks of much music. Besides containing an organized set of pitches on which to base a tune, they can be particularly useful in soloing, an area where the keyboard player gets to show off. Knowing one's scales (how they are formed, and what pitches make up each scale), and being able to *play* the scales are two different things. From a compositional standpoint, it may be important to understand scale construction and origin, but in the area of playing, all scales must be fluid underneath the fingers, without having to think about them. This will be discussed in greater detail later under "soloing," but for now, several scales and methods of practicing them will be presented in order to build up your technique in this area.

Major

The **major scale** consists of seven different pitches, arranged in a particular order of half (H) and whole (W) steps: WWHWWWH. When starting on C, this gives us all white keys from C to C. Beginning on G gives us all white keys except on F, where F♯ is used instead.

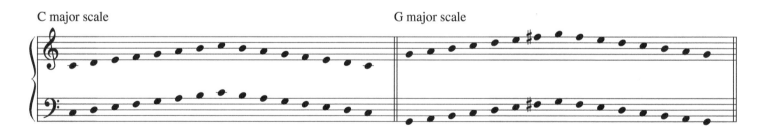

C major scale   G major scale

Scales include progressively more black keys as we go through the **circle of fifths**. For more on this topic, as well as key signatures and scale construction, please see Mark Harrison's *Contemporary Music Theory*, Levels 1–3 (Hal Leonard Corporation). For now, the following system of scale practice will help ensure that you get these moving smoothly and effortlessly in your hands, so that you no longer need to think about them.

We will begin with the C major scale. Start with the hands separately, playing one octave, up and down. Follow the fingerings, and practice with a metronome to help keep things even. Notice how in ascending with the right hand, the thumb will cross underneath the hand after the first three notes to play F. After that, the other fingers should line up with G–A–B–C. The left-hand finger 3 (middle finger) will cross over after the thumb has played G. On the way down, each hand employs the same finger crossing as the opposite hand did on the way up.

When you are comfortable with this at a tempo of ♩ = 120, put the hands together. This may be tricky at first since the finger crossings do not occur at the same place between the hands—go very slowly (♩ = 60 or less)! Once you can play the scale three times in a row without error, turn the metronome up two notches and do it again. Repeat this process until you reach the goal tempo of 120.

The next step is a scale exercise that you can play as a warm up for the rest of your life. This will help develop speed and fluidity, as well as warm up the fingers for a performance. This exercise involves playing the scales, hands together, multiple octaves. First, the scale is played two octaves up and down using eighth notes, accenting every other note. In doing this, you will notice that the accents occur on different notes and different fingers in the second octave. When you return back to "home," you will immediately start the scale again, but this time playing triplets, accenting every fourth note, and going up and down three octaves. Finally, the last scale will be played four octaves at sixteenth notes, accenting every fifth note. The entire exercise is notated in the following example using the C major scale. Finger numbers are given only at the places where there is a thumb turn or a finger crossing over, and only for the first octave of the scale. The same fingering pattern applies for the rest of the exercise. Use a metronome!

TRACK 52

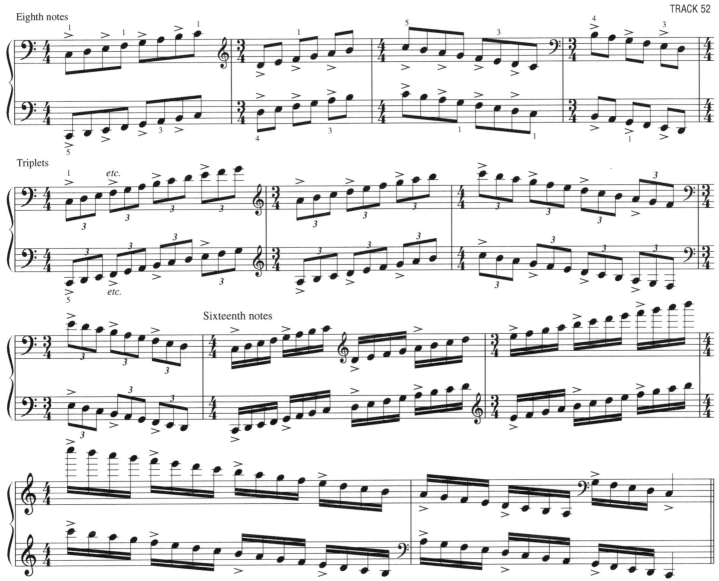

NOTE: Watch out for the clef changes and meter changes; these make it look more complicated than it really is. Listen to the track and play along. Once you get used to the pattern, you won't need to read this, and can use it for all major scales.

The accents and rhythmic changes have many applications in "real" music. Practice this with all the major scales. While several of the major scales can be played with the same fingering as the C major scale, several others use different fingerings. For complete scales and fingerings, please consult a scale chart or exercise book.

Minor

There are three **minor scales**: natural, harmonic, and melodic. The **natural minor** is derived by simply taking the major scale and beginning it on a different note. Each major scale has a relative minor that comes from the sixth degree of the scale. Since the sixth note of the C major scale is A, A minor is relative to C major. One can practice the natural minor scales the same as the major. Since the order of notes has changed, some of the fingerings may as well. In the A natural minor scale below, the fingerings are exactly the same as the C major scale.

The **harmonic minor** scale is the same as the natural minor, but with the seventh degree raised by a half step to provide a leading tone.

A harmonic minor

The origins of this scale come from the fact that, in minor keys, the V chord is naturally a minor triad. In order to turn this chord into a dominant functioning chord (one that "wants" to lead back to I), it must be made major, thereby raising the third of the chord (the seventh degree of the scale/key). In A minor, the V chord is an E chord. Raising the third, G, to G♯ gives us an E major chord. This change from the natural version of the scale results from *harmonic* tendencies that occur in tonal music, thus a scale with this change results in the harmonic minor scale. Though this scale was conceived more for theoretical purposes, its unique and exotic sound (due to the augmented 2nd between the sixth and seventh degrees) became used compositionally, and in soloing. Practicing the scale can help bring about unique compositional ideas in your jam sessions, or provide for a distinctive sound in your solos.

The **melodic minor** scale has origins similar to those of the harmonic's, but for reasons of melody instead of harmony. In common-practice tonal music, we already noted how the V chord was made major in pieces in a minor key. In melody, an ascending approach to the tonic is made more meaningful when the tonic is preceded by its leading tone (a half step away). Raising the seventh degree to provide for a leading tone, creates the exotic sounding interval of the augmented 2nd between the sixth and seventh degrees. In older times, this exoticism was viewed as improper, and not "real" music. So in order to make this melodic movement sound smoother, the sixth scale degree was also raised, "correcting" the augmented 2nd to a major 2nd. Thus the difference between a major scale and a melodic minor scale is only that the third degree is lower in the minor.

A melodic minor

Again, using this scale in soloing or other melodic lines can produce a different sound from that of the natural minor. Practice this scale in all keys as you would the major scale.

Scalar passages in general, especially when played quickly, can help add just the right amount of virtuosic display. In progressive metal, it is common for the keys and guitar to engage in quick scalar passages in unison, or in parallel harmony, usually a third or sixth apart.

The following example shows a scalar-based keyboard solo in the progressive metal style utilizing the E natural minor scale. On the audio, the guitar solo is in parallel harmony with the keyboard solo, mostly a 3rd below. To hear only the keyboard solo with the rhythm section, turn down the left channel on your stereo.

This sounds impressive and difficult, but for anyone who has practiced scales diligently, a passage like this is well within the realm of possibility. If you follow the suggested fingering, you'll notice that everything "lays" well in the fingers and is fairly easy to play. Notice the fingering at the end: the second to last note (E) is played with finger 5, then the last note, the same pitch, is played with 3. When repeating notes, especially in fast passages, it is a good idea to use different fingers. The third finger is chosen for the last note so as to end with strength.

Octave scales

A common keyboard technique redolent of showmanship, stemming from some of the great romantic-era composers, is the use of scales in octaves. This is possible with any scale. In all cases, the scale will be played with an octave doubling in the same hand as in the following.

The bottom note is played with the thumb, and the top with the little finger (vice versa in the left hand). This should be played somewhat staccato, in a bouncing manner to move more easily from one note to the next. As with all scales, practice the hands separately first, then put them together.

The next example demonstrates a piano solo employing the flamboyant doubled-octave technique as heard in solos by Rick Wakeman, Keith Emerson, Jordan Rudess, and many other progressive rock keyboard virtuosos.

8vb - ⌐

Notice how, when the left hand plays an octave scale figure, it is either in parallel harmony with the right hand, or in contrary motion to the right hand.

Make sure when employing this technique that you keep your finger-spread rigid, and don't bounce your hand too high. It's easy to hit the wrong note(s), so practice slowly, and aim for accuracy. Also, if you're reading, you may find it helpful to memorize the passage so you can look down at your hands.

Pentatonic

As the prefix of this scale indicates, this is a five-note collection. There are two basic types: the major pentatonic, and the minor pentatonic. The **major pentatonic** consists of five pitches of the major scale: the first, second, third, fifth, and sixth degrees. In C major, this would yield C, D, E, G, A.

C major pentatonic

This arrangement leaves us with no minor seconds, allowing for a more open sound, one that does not have a tendency to "lead" anywhere. The **minor pentatonic** consists of the same intervals, but in a different order. If we take the relative minor of C major (which is A minor), we simply use the same pitches as the relative major, but begin with A: A, C, D, E, G. When comparing this to the scale degrees of the natural minor scale, we see that these pitches are the first, third, fourth, fifth, and seventh degrees.

A minor pentatonic

These scales are commonly used for soloing, not only in progressive rock, but in rock music in general, as well as in jazz, blues, and many other styles. The pentatonic scale is also connected to Asian music, and many groups, wishing to give an exotic quality to a tune, have employed this scale in melodies. The black keys of the keyboard themselves make up a pentatonic scale (an F#/G♭ major or D#/E♭ minor pentatonic). This scale also serves a connection to another important scale, perhaps the most important in rock 'n' roll: the blues scale.

Blues

The **blues scale** can be constructed by taking the minor pentatonic and adding one more pitch, a raised fourth degree. An A blues scale is shown in the next example which consists of the A minor pentatonic, plus D#.

A blues scale

Many progressive rock bands employ the blues scale in melodies and soloing. With much of prog having a classical music influence, the employment of the blues scale helps inject it with a bit of rock 'n' roll, making it less "stuffy" perhaps.

The next example takes Bach's "Two-Part Invention No. 7 in E Minor" and alters it. By changing a few pitches here and there to conform to the blues scale, we add a bit of "rock" to the tune. Example **A** shows an excerpt from the original while Example **B** shows our "rocked up" version. The changed pitches have been indicated in Example **B**. **Track 55** plays the original Bach piece while **Track 56** plays the altered version. **Track 57** plays the altered version using an organ sound for the right hand, and a Moog sound for the left hand (sounding an octave lower than written), backed up by the full band so you can hear it in a full rock context.

Two-Part Invention No. 7 in E Minor

(Original)

TRACK 55
rock, piano only

Johann Sebastian Bach

Two-Part Invention No. 7 in E Minor

(Altered "Rock/Blues" Version)

TRACK 56
Rock, piano-only

TRACK 57
Rock, full band

Johann Sebastian Bach

* = changed or added notes

Grace notes have been included as an embellishment of the fifth scale degree, B. In certain places, where we have the pitch B in the original, the rock version ornaments this pitch with a grace note a half step below. In your own keyboard playing, experiment with the blues scale by taking classical-sounding passages and adding a few **blue notes**: the raised fourth, for example. This is a great way to use some of the classical music structures, yet keep the music rockin'. In jazz and blues, the term "blue note" may also refer to, with reference to the major scale, the lowered third and lowered seventh, in addition to the raised fourth (sometimes deemed a lowered fifth).

Octatonic/Diminished

This scale was discussed in Chapter 4 as a compositional device. If you desire to take your music "outside" a bit, this scale can be used in tonal as well as atonal contexts. The following example shows all three octatonic scales. Fingering is a bit trickier since the scale contains eight instead of seven pitches, but there are several possibilities. Also, since these are symmetrical scales, practice beginning the scale on different pitches within the collection. Figure out fingerings that work best for you, and practice these scales, starting on different pitches, always using the same fingering. This will help ensure that, say, in an improvised solo, when you are using one of these scales, your fingers will move quickly and smoothly because they are accustomed to certain fingering patterns.

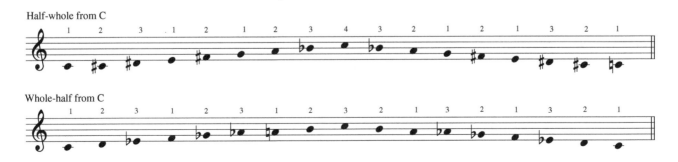

Once you have these comfortable and fluid underneath your fingers, you can begin to experiment using them in musical contexts. The following example shows one of many possibilities. The tune is in D minor, and the piano solo begins using the D minor scale for the first four measures. In measure five, the octatonic scale is employed to take the solo further outside. Such use is common in jazz as well as some of the more adventurous progressive rock.

TRACK 58

In this case, the octatonic scale chosen was the half-whole beginning on C. The pitch D is purposefully missing as a way to take it "outside." Yet to keep is somewhat grounded, the dominant scale degree of the key (A) is used in places such as the end or beginning of phrases or licks.

Whole tone

Another atonal scale discussed in Chapter 4, the whole tone, works well for melodic lines over augmented triads, or any other sonorities that come from the notes of the whole tone scale, such as a dominant seventh chord with the fifth omitted. The following shows the two whole tone scales along with possible fingerings. The first scale is accompanied by an augmented triad in the left hand, while the second scale is played against a dominant seventh chord.

Getting any and all scales to a level where you can play them quickly and evenly, without thinking about them, will aid your playing greatly, especially when it comes to soloing, whether pre-composed or improvised. One could effectively use several different types of scale even with a piece/section that stays in the same key. The next example is in E minor, but besides the E natural minor scale, the keyboard solo also uses the B minor (using a scale based on the fifth degree of a key is a common substitution), whole tone, and octatonic scales, each of which is bracketed in the example.

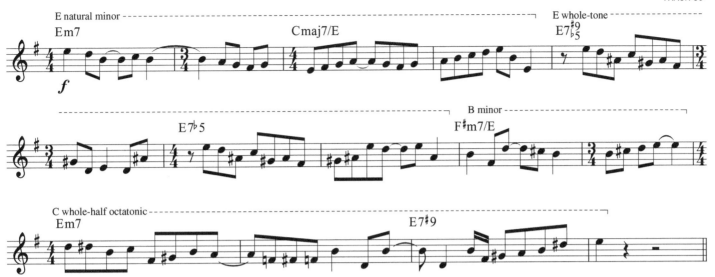

As you can see, knowing multiple scales and being able to play them effortlessly allows you to be able to switch from one to the next to create interesting melodic lines and solos.

Arpeggios

Arpeggios (arps) are chords whose pitches are sounded successively rather than simultaneously. Meaning "harp" (an instrument known for playing lots of arps), this technique can be executed in a variety of ways for many different purposes. The following demonstrates a simple C minor arp, spanning one octave, played with one hand.

Playing arps in this way, one can use one hand, without any finger crossing. Next, we see the same Cm arp begin a I–IV–V7–I chord progression, with the hand barely moving. Try this first at a slow tempo, then gradually speed it up.

Try this in a variety of chord progressions, in multiple keys.

Next, we have the same arpeggio progression, but utilizing both hands. This increases the harp-like effect, extending the sonic landscape.

Depending on speed, dynamics, and timbre, arps can constitute part of an "in your face" element, as heard in solos by many of the "shredder-type" guitar heroes, or they can also be used in a more subtle way as a background "wash" effect. In the next example, quickly-played arpeggios are used as background behind an acoustic guitar solo. A thinner organ patch keeps the sound soft and light. This one is in the style of Yes.

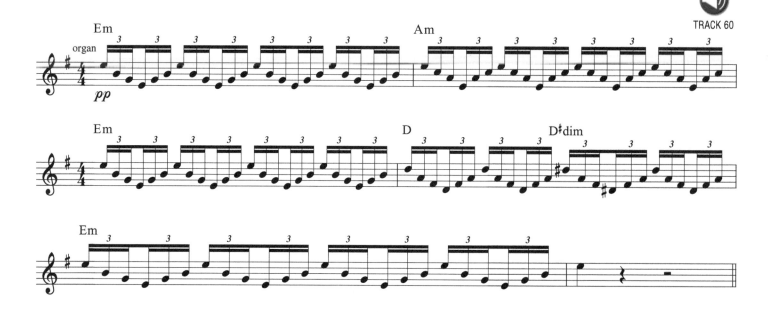

You may practice chord progressions of all types with arpeggios. Besides progressions, one can go up and down the scale, playing arps from each scale degree.

Arpeggio scale exercise – E natural minor

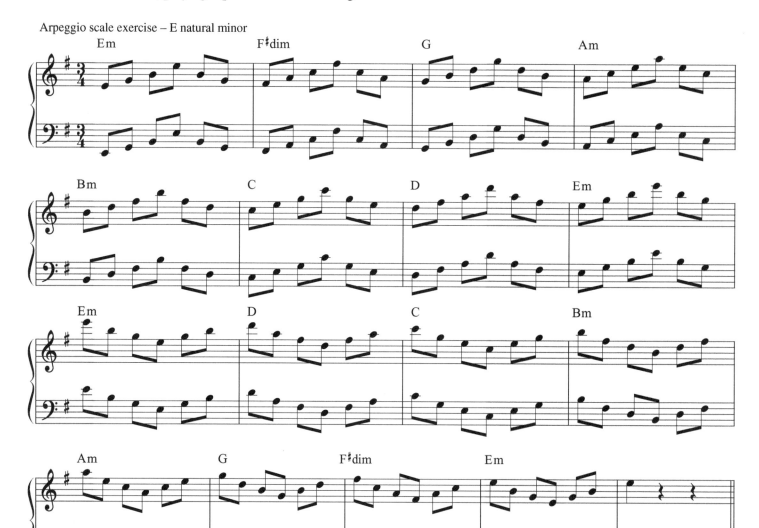

This is a great exercise to practice on all scales, in all keys. Practice hands separately, then together. Use a metronome and work on maintaining evenness.

For a more advanced technique, each hand will travel two octaves, employing finger crossing. Sticking with our E minor arps, we'll first focus on the right hand. Make sure that the right thumb begins to turn under as soon as it is done playing the first note. It should turn and aim for the next E, an octave above the starting note, and when it reaches the E and plays it, the other fingers snap into place to keep playing up the arpeggio. On the way down, as the thumb plays the E, the whole hand pivots on the thumb with the third finger crossing over, aiming for the B. Though the following example only shows this in two octaves, this technique can be used for any number of octaves.

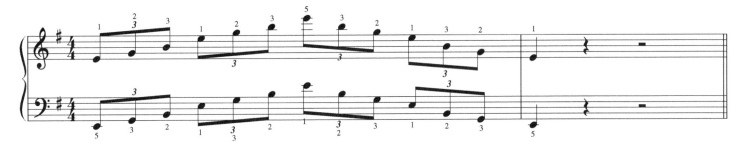

You should also practice this exercise in the left hand, following the same concepts of pivoting the hand and crossing the third finger ahead of time on the way up, as well as turning the thumb underneath on the way down. Once you have each hand learned separately, try them together.

Finally, we see a common flourish where the arps travel up and down much of the length of the keyboard. Such a device can be used within solos to end or begin phrases, but caution should be exercised in employing this too often during any one particular solo. Such overuse can become predictable and mechanical. In executing this technique, it is important that once a hand is done playing, that hand moves quickly to the next position (crossing over the other hand) while the other hand is playing. This ensures a smooth arpeggio without pause or hesitation. Practice this as an exercise in various chord progressions and scales to develop technique, but in actual musical playing (soloing) be careful not to overdo it. In the following example, the left-hand notes are always in the lower staff, and the right-hand notes in the upper. Watch out for the clef changes.

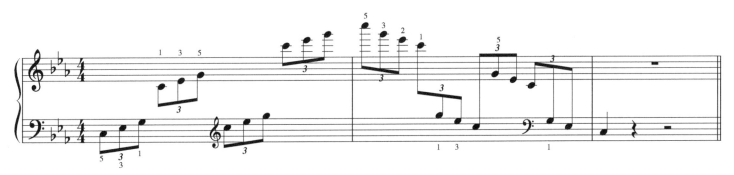

As with finger crossings and thumb turns, the hand should cross over as soon as it is done playing so it is ready, in position by the time the other hand finishes playing its notes.

All of the above exercises and techniques should be done using all chords in all keys. Also, make your practicing fun by creating your own progressions, as well as your own unique exercises. Learning patterns such as these, and practicing them the same way each time (the same fingering) will help you to execute quick and clean arpeggios in your solos and accompaniment parts. Such creativity will not only make practicing more enjoyable, but may also spawn musical ideas to be refined and developed in your composing or soloing.

The last example in this section features a short solo utilizing a combination of scales and arpeggios. This serves as just one small demonstration of what is possible from the practice of a few simple exercises in these techniques.

This solo is almost exclusively for the right hand. But remember to practice all exercises equally in both hands (or more in the weaker hand). When the left and right hand are both used in soloing, many more possibilities are available for either additional harmony, or methods of executing even faster scales and arpeggios, some of what we've seen possible when one hand crosses over the other.

The process of consciously combining various scales and arpeggios to create a solo may seem very academic—it is. If you look at/listen to some of the great keyboard solos in progressive rock, you will definitely hear these items within the solos. However, players rarely, if ever, consciously think to themselves and design their solos or melodies based on a careful "putting together" of various scale and arpeggio patterns. The previous exercises are meant to serve as tools for developing your musical vocabulary. When these items are practiced and learned well enough to be executed without thought, they eventually become more of a natural and intuitive part of your playing. The many scales and arps you can play meld with your creativity, instinct, and spontaneity, thereby expanding your overall playing abilities, both in composing and improvising.

Independence

This section focuses on techniques that involve each hand doing something entirely different from the other, simultaneously. Such playing requires very slow practice, with a metronome.

Contrapuntal playing

In Chapter 5, we discussed the importance of counterpoint as a compositional device, one that separates progressive rock from other rock 'n' roll. Playing contrapuntal parts on the keyboard can be a challenge, but it is a must for any prog keyboardist. A good way to get your technique in shape is by playing the J.S. Bach "Two-Part Inventions." We've seen excerpts from a few of these already, in Chapter 5 and earlier in this chapter. Pick up a book that includes all of the Two-Part Inventions in one volume, and make sure to get a version with finger numbers included. Each Invention offers at least slightly different challenges to help develop overall technique. The pieces also cover a number of keys to improve versatility in multiple tonalities.

Practice these with a metronome, hands separately at first. Go through one phrase (2–4 measures) at a time. When one hand is solid, practice the other hand, the same phrase. Next, put the hands together, setting the metronome at a slow enough tempo to enable you to play the entire phrase, without error. Now, this may be ridiculously slow, but keep it up. When you can play the phrase three times in a row, without a mistake, turn the metronome faster by two notches (BPM), and repeat the process until the phrase is at the proper tempo. It is also important to overlap your phrases. For example, end your practice-run two beats into the next phrase. When you are ready to practice the next phrase, you will be starting with the last two beats of what you just practiced. This helps ensure that when you string all the phrases together, you will avoid pauses and hesitations at phrase breaks.

Bass line/Ostinato and solo

One keyboardist known for covering a lot of territory on the keys with respect to orchestration is Keith Emerson. Since ELP was a trio without guitar, the keyboard parts were able take advantage of filling in a lot of space. However, doing so can be another great challenge to the keyboardist. Filling in space often requires great independence between the hands as we have seen in contrapuntal playing. For instance, this may demand that the keyboardist player play a bass line **ostinato** (short, repeated pattern) with the left hand while the right hand plays the melody/solo. The following example, in the style of ELP, demonstrates the keys in this role.

TRACK 62

In practicing such figures, make sure the ostinato is solid. It must be memorized so that executing the pattern requires no thought—this becomes the mechanical part of playing. In doing so, the mind and right hand are free to play expressively, perhaps improvising while the left hand is on "automatic pilot." Once the ostinato is mastered, begin by playing scales in the right hand, in eighth notes, along with the ostinato in the left hand. Use a metronome, and work slowly.

The previous example may be too difficult to start out with, especially when the ostinato is in an odd meter (or even changing meter). Before jumping into ELP-styled keyboard parts, the following exercises can help you get started with this technique.

The following example is a simpler ostinato in 4/4 time. The right hand simply plays a two-octave scale up and down. When practicing this type of exercise, start out by playing a couple bars of the ostinato by itself.

The challenging part to playing an ostinato like this is the syncopation (the note on the "and" of 2, tied to beat 3). Many ostinatos will have some sort of syncopation, because it is in the nature of an ostinato to be rhythmically interesting in some way.

You should also compose your own ostinatos and practice scales in all keys (as well as synthetic scales: octatonic, whole tone, etc.) along with your patterns.

The next ostinato exercise shows the right hand playing a melody, along with the same ostinato from the previous example.

Next, we get to something even more challenging. Below, the ostinato is in the right hand while the left hand plays the scale.

The previous examples should also be adapted to your own ostinatos, in many different keys and harmonic schemes. Give equal (or more) treatment to your left hand for increased skill. Having an agile left hand can improve your ability to play impressive lines, whether the left hand plays them by itself, or is used to aid and enhance something the right hand is playing.

Next, the ostinato is in an odd meter (5/8), like the previous ELP-like example. Also note that, when playing scales in different meters, you can change the rhythm and/or repeat notes (like the tonic, once you reach the top of the scale) to make the scale "fit" nicely into metrical groups.

This next exercise exhibits changing meter, again in the style of ELP. The alternation between 5/8, 2/4, 5/8, and 3/4 can prove to be a challenge; however, once the pattern becomes automatic, it will leave your right hand free to solo. The left hand is played using a piano sound while the right hand uses a Hammond organ sound.

In much progressive rock, catchy ostinatos, often in an odd or changing meter patterns, make the genre instantly identifiable, with ELP's contributions pioneering this aspect of prog.

Try all of the above ostinatos with scales, improvised soloing, and melodies you compose. Also, reverse the hands on all examples: the right hand playing the ostinato while the left hand plays the melody. In addition, if you have more than one keyboard (or if you can split your keyboard), try the left hand on an organ, and the right hand on a lead synth. Experiment with many of these types of combinations. This will not only make practice fun, but can produce some compositional ideas for your own tunes. Such practice will also go a long way in developing great chops, offering opportunities to fill in a lot of musical space.

Multiple sounds and keyboard instruments

One of the demanding requirements of the prog keyboardist is being able to cover multiple roles at the same time. These roles include playing the melody, bass line, and inner voices/harmony. In progressive rock, one way to take this even further is not only to play all roles at the same time, but to play each part with a different sound. For example, while the right hand plays a melody on the Moog or lead synth, the left hand could play a bass line or chordal accompaniment on an organ. In addition, at certain points when either hand gets a quick break, chords can be sounded on a Mellotron or other synth, and held with the pedal. This technique covers a lot of ground, filling up the sound spectrum with only one player.

The following example shows the left hand playing a chordal accompaniment on the organ while the right hand goes back and forth between playing a melody on the piano (question or **antecedent** phrase) and a melody on a lead synth patch (answer or **consequent** phrase).

TRACK 64

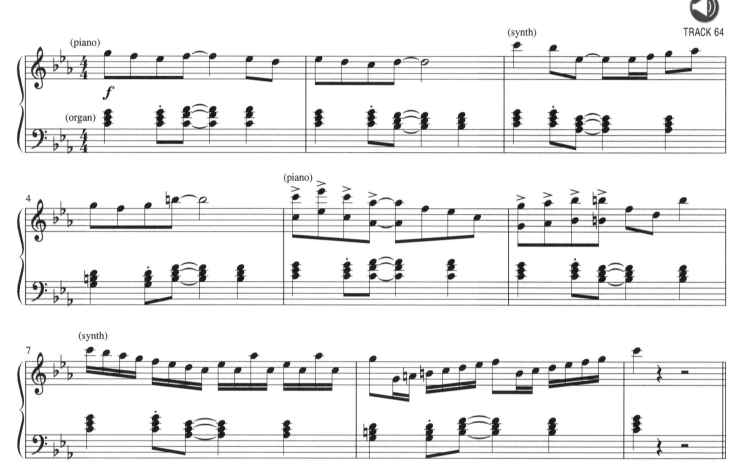

Notice how the end of each phrase (or semi-phrase) ends with a longer note. This allows the player time to move the hand to the next sound to play the next phrase.

In ideal situations, the player would have three keyboards to execute this, though it can be done easily with two. Players like Rick Wakeman have been known to surround themselves with ten or more keyboards, often stacked in multiple vertical layers. It may be helpful to rent one of his solo concert videos and watch as he moves quickly from one to the next, often playing two or three different instruments at the same time.

Since we're all not wealthy enough to afford ten (or even three) keyboards, other possibilities exist. Many modern synthesizers offer "split keyboard" functions. To play the previous example with two keyboards, one could set the instrument so the organ patch is assigned to the bottom half of the keyboard, while the top half holds the piano sound. To play the synth "answer" phrases, a second keyboard would be assigned that patch and be positioned either above or below the first keyboard on a double-tier stand. Or one keyboard could sound the organ, played by the left hand, and the other keyboard could be split, one half programmed with the piano sound and the other half the synth sound. Playing this passage with only one keyboard is also possible. To do this, a quick patch change would be necessary from piano to synth. Such changes are a necessary part of the prog keyboardist's playing technique. Many modern synthesizers offer easy and quick custom programming capabilities. For example, you could have a patch ready to go that splits your keyboard in many different combinations. You can then change from one custom setting to another by just the quick push of a button. One can also get pedals that operate via MIDI to change patches quickly with the feet, without ever having to stop the hands from playing.

If you are composing and creating keyboard parts, you can tailor your synthesizer settings to your specific needs. The "chops" element comes in with regard to practice. Once you have your parts composed, and you know what combinations of sounds you'll be using, including changing from one sound to another, you must then practice making these changes in real time. Traditional piano playing does not take into consideration having to change sounds while playing, but in progressive rock, the art of changing between sounds quickly becomes another facet of the virtuosity. Once you get this learned, it becomes automatic. The more you practice this, the more you will be able to make yourself sound like a small orchestra, helping enhance your band's progressive sound.

You can also approach this from a different angle: Set up your keyboard(s) featuring a few different types of sounds, split, and/or layered, and improvise with these settings. As part of your improvisation, initiate some quick patch changes when the mood strikes you. This kind of activity can help generate ideas and create keyboard parts as well as entire compositions.

Lead Synth Techniques: Special-Effect Expressions

With the advent of digital synthesizers, keyboard players could apply devices such as **pitch bend**, **vibrato**, and **tremolo**, all with the use of a joystick or wheel, usually located just to the left of the lowest key on the keyboard. Such effects allowed the player more opportunities for expression, often simulating what could be done on guitar, or even orchestral string instruments. Pitch bend is usually executed by moving the stick left and right, while vibrato is achieved by moving it up. Moving the stick down can employ tremolo. Other devices are common such as a wheel instead of a joystick. Some wheels are sensitive to pressure (pushing down on the wheel to produce vibrato). Whatever your keyboard has, the functions of the wheel or stick are often programmable.

Note Bends

Many synths allow you to program the interval of the bend produced by the pitch-bend wheel or joystick. Most commonly, notes are bent up or down to the next pitch in the scale, thus either a whole step or a half step. For the following exercise, set the bend interval to a whole step. Practice bending the note, in rhythm as notated. When the music indicates to bend the note a whole step, simply move the wheel as far as it goes in the proper direction. Work on reaching the target note exactly on beat 3 as in example **A**. Example **B** requires that the note only be bent a half step. This requires a bit more aural skill. Test out the target pitch by playing it first to get the sound in your head. Next, practice bending to it, listening carefully to reach the pitch, yet not go beyond it. Enough practice of this will eventually get you used to the feel of it as well as using your ears. The bend is notated as a wavy line from the starting note to the target note.

TRACK 65

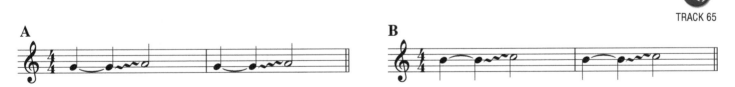

The next example shows a simple melody with whole-step and half-step bends, some up, some down. Upon reaching the desired note at the end of the bend, you must quickly let go of the wheel immediately before the next note so as not to hear the effect on the following notes.

Practice bending up, down, and up then down, as in the previous example. Though practice can help you get used to the feel of bending, the real issue is when and where to bend. It's easy to overdo it, so use note bending cautiously. Bending up or down to longer notes that end phrases can work well, but that doesn't mean that a quick bend between two notes in the middle of a phrase can't also be effective. Use your best artistic judgement.

To be more adventurous, you can set the pitch-bend wheel to an octave and practice bending any intervals within this span. This takes a lot of practice and good ears since the sensitivity of the pitch bend wheel makes it tricky to lock into specific pitches in the middle of a bend. Hitting these intervals exactly, especially in fast tempos/rhythms is difficult. However, with careful practice, it can be achieved. Choose carefully where you want to employ bends larger than a major second. Most often, the pitch bend is set to the major second, where bends between adjacent scale degrees are easily executed to add to the expressiveness of a melody or solo.

The next example features a melody including several bends for added expression. On the track, the first example plays the melody without the bends; this is followed by a performance of the melody with all the bends included. Listen for the expressive difference between the two.

TRACK 67

Vibrato and tremolo

Vibrato is used by numerous wind and string players to help promote a "singing tone." This consists of a regular, but slight bending of the pitch, both above and below the original note. The wheel used for the pitch bend usually has a vibrato function also. Many synths allow the user to program how far the pitch is bent in the vibrato, as well as how fast the bending up and down occurs. Also, how far up you move the stick can determine how much (how fast and/or how wide) vibrato is employed. This allows for more control, allowing for your vibrato to have variances, sounding less mechanical.

In the next example, we take our previous melody and add vibrato on certain notes. Vibrato is rarely notated (but it is shown here for demonstration purposes with a "v" above the notes)—and players usually employ it by feel. It commonly ends up being used on longer notes to end phrases or semi-phrases, but can be used anywhere. Listen to the next track, which demonstrates our original simple melody, with the bends, and now with vibrato added to make it fully expressive. This is an advantage over the piano, which is incapable of such expressions.

Though most of the vibrato has been employed on the longer, phrase-ending notes, you can hear that some was used on shorter notes, as in the fifth complete measure. Here, the vibrato is employed quickly as an accent-like effect. As with all special effects, be careful not to overuse this technique—less is more.

The last example is in the style of Dream Theater, and makes use of vibrato and pitch bending. Listen for the singing quality, not far from what a violinist might play.

Chapter 7
FORM AND DEVELOPMENT

This chapter focuses more on the compositional portion of the book rather than the performance. If one wishes to create their own progressive rock tunes, a solid basis in formal design can go a long way in helping to achieve this. There is a lot of prog out there which only captures the superficial elements of the genre such as changing meter, syncopated rhythms, instrumental virtuosity, busy counterpoint, mood changes, and varied instrumentation. All these items are important, but like a house made of cards—albeit very beautiful, elegant, fancy cards—tunes such as these will only provide the listener with frosting, and little substance, thereby failing to capture their long-term interest. The following will help the progressive rock composer and keyboard player to create and play parts that have an overall meaning and relationship to the whole.

Definition

Musical **form** is the overall structure of a musical work—how smaller parts are put together to make a larger whole. This is construed as something apart from, or at least larger than, the "contents," consisting of individual notes, melodies, dynamics, and all smaller details. How one describes or labels a form depends on how general one wishes to be. For example, a very simple label of a form could be based on mood: I – Angry, II – Sad, III – Excited. These three basic moods could be considered a formal design. Tempo and dynamics can also describe form: I – Medium & Loud, II – Slow & Quiet, III – Fast & Very Loud.

In "The Trees" by Rush, the music may be heard to have three major parts, plus an introduction:

Intro: classical guitar and voice – quiet

Part I: driving rock with vocals – loud

Part II: quiet, atmospheric, with keyboard solo

Part III: return to style of Part I

In this common "loud-soft-loud" formula, the keyboards are offered the chance to shine in the middle section. Compared to pop music, this is sometimes viewed as an expanded or extended song form. It has the simpler verse–chorus song structure, but inserts an (often) instrumental interlude in the middle, a section usually of a contrasting mood. This form increases the dramatic quality of the tune by offering a simulation of more than one setting, akin to a movie taking place in a multitude of settings as opposed to a sitcom taking place in one or two locations. The next example is in the style of the middle section of "The Trees." The keyboard solo is similar to a woodwind solo in an orchestral piece. Instead of a solo section that is loud and fast like the rest of the tune, following the same chord progression and accompaniment as the chorus or verse (as in many rock songs), this solo is set in a truly different section of music.

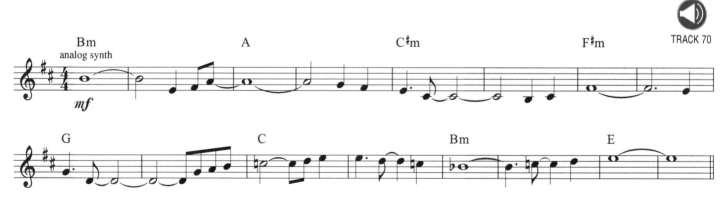

On a more detailed level, one may think of form as the plot of a story. Individual characters and what they do are part of the contents that make up the plot. There can be many different types of plots, but all have a few items in common. The concepts of **tension** and **release**, as well as **repetition** and **variation** are what drive the plot forward. A story may involve several main characters. From beginning to end, these characters go through experiences that contribute to growth. By the end of the story, provided they are alive, they are still the same people (or dogs, cats, elves, dragons, etc.), but people who have grown, learned, and changed throughout the storyline. This development may be anything from small to catastrophic, but at least some semblance of the same characters remains. **Tension** may be represented by a problem for a character to resolve with the **release** being the solution. **Repetition** may involve character traits: a certain character is likely to act or react to situations of tension in certain ways each time. If some action does not help solve the problem, the action is varied and attempted again (**variation**).

The musical form of a composition has a lot to do with the events in a storyline, and its effect on the characters. The impact of events plays a major role. The setting of the story is also a major part of the form.

Progressive rock is often described as being complex. This complexity is one of the major attractions of the genre, that which engages the listener, helping to develop long-term devoted fans. But what is complexity? Chapter 5 discussed counterpoint, a musical device that can often make a tune *sound* complex. What is often heard in prog is a certain kind of busyness, with many different parts playing at the same time. When these parts are executed by highly skilled players, it sounds complex. However, we should be careful not to confuse busyness with complexity. What you will find is that "good" music has multiple levels. A tune could have many elements, all working at the same time, overlapping, etc. What makes it complex is not the number of levels, or even how they sound together, but how well these multiple levels *relate* to each other, and to the whole.

The complexity of much classical music comes from the form and the depth of the relationships within. Progressive rock often mimics these forms. Going back to the story analogy, we will use television/film as an example. Formally speaking, pop rock may be seen as the sitcom, whereas prog is the two-hour psychological thriller (or other "mind-bending" genre). We've all seen sitcoms that follow the same formula for every episode—music often does the same. How, when, and where musical items such as themes and motifs are re-stated and developed helps give a tune its formal shape.

Tension and Release/ Repetition and Variation

There are many ways to create tension and release in music. Dissonant or unstable harmonies resolving to more consonant or stable harmonies is one simple process that helps promote motion in a lot of music. In Chapter 4 we learned of the instability of the dominant seventh chord—the interval between the third and seventh produces the dissonant tritone, which if spelled as an augmented 4th resolves outward to a 6th, and if spelled as a diminished 5th resolves inward to a 3rd. This is a standard move in tonal music, one at the heart of its harmonic vocabulary.

The dominant seventh chord can also be used in a slightly more unexpected manner, resolving to something other than its I chord. The tension of the tritone can move outwards (by half step), resolving to a chord only a half step away. Below we see a G dominant seventh chord, one that would normally resolve to C. If, instead of resolving the tritone between B and F inwards to C and E, we move the interval outward to A♯ and F♯, we arrive at an F♯ chord.

This move still provides for a satisfying release in that the dissonant tritone resolves by half step in both directions. The surprise element comes from the fact that the chord to which it resolves is a tritone away from the C chord, the "expected" resolution. To install further tension and release, the following example will put this move into context. The first four measures see a standard I–IV–I–V progression returning to I in the fifth measure. **Repetition** occurs when the music returns to the same progression, playing the same piano part. **Variation** occurs when the G7 chord in the second progression is prolonged, letting the dissonance establish increased tension, producing a greater desire in the listener to hear the return to C. When the G7 resolves to the F♯ instead, there is a great release, but an unexpected one. Both this resolution and the surprising nature of the F♯ chord are enhanced by the prolongation of the G7 through repetition.

TRACK 71

In strict theory terms, a G7 chord resolving outward to an F♯ chord would be spelled G, B, D, E♯, and would be labeled an **augmented sixth** chord. If you're interested in more about "strict" theory, please consult a theory text on this subject. For the sake of your progressive rock keyboard playing and composing, the important thing is to be aware of this outward resolution of the tritone and how it can produce a release that is both satisfying and unexpected.

A **chromatic mediant** (see Chapter 4) move can also provide a source of release, offering unexpected change to a preceding repetition. The next example features a piano part in the style of Kansas, and uses a piano sound layered with organ (a simple patch to create on most synthesizers, and a signature prog sound in bands like Kansas). The verse-like section is divided into two parts that contrast each other in several ways. The first part (measures 1–6) is comprised of two statements of a three-bar progression in A major, with the pitch A functioning as a pedal tone in the bass (another source of repetition). In measure 7, the music moves to a C major triad (launching a progression in C major), a chromatic mediant of A, our main tonality, and also a chromatic mediant of the E chord that precedes it. This somewhat unexpected harmonic shift, coupled with a change to 5/8 meter, provides for a release to the repetitive progression in A.

Notice an additional element of repetition, a connecting relationship between the two phrases: both the A major and C major progressions end with an E major chord. This not only provides for a similarity between the two, promoting unity through commonality, but would also allow for the C progression to return to A (E is the dominant of A). Each of these elements (the chromatic mediant and the 5/8 meter) by themselves may be seen in a wide variety of rock and pop music, but the combination of both tactics makes this a bit more adventurous, and more uniquely progressive rock. Also note the same type of arpeggio used at the end of both phrases (measures 3 and 6 in the A major phrases, and measures 10 and 14 in the C major phrases).

Other methods of repetition and variation include various treatments of musical ideas. The following terms are used to describe some of these treatments: **retrograde**, **inversion**, **augmentation**, **diminution**, and **fragmentation**. All of these methods represent ways of varying material such as themes/melodies, chord progressions, and rhythmic motives. Although these methods may seem like academic exercises, it is through experimentation with them (actually "trying them out") that you may find interesting results that work well in your playing and composing. They provide a way to use and reuse material without literally repeating it. Repetition is necessary for music to have cohesion and "make sense," but literal repetition can become tiresome. Whether you're composing whole tunes or just your own keyboard parts, the following methods will help keep your ideas fresh, interesting, and even surprising, while maintaining overall unity that is needed for the tune to "work."

Retrograde

Retrograde is a fancy term for "backwards." Simply playing a melody backwards is an example. Although listeners may not consciously perceive that they are hearing the main melody of a tune backwards, a relationship may be perceived subconsciously. Experiment with your melodies—sometimes a theme played backwards results in an equally interesting and catchy melody in itself. If not, reversed melodies can be used for background material, bass lines, or may even work as counterpoint to other melodies.

The following example takes a melody, and reverses the pitches, but keeps the same rhythm. Compare both melodies and listen for similarities and differences.

Melody 1

Melody 2 (retrograde pitches, same rhythm)

Rhythms themselves can be reversed as well. The following melody is presented in two versions. The second takes the same pitches (in the same order) as the first, but simply plays them utilizing the reverse rhythm.

Melody 1

Melody 3 (retrograde rhythm, same pitches)

The next example shows a full retrograde (pitches and rhythm of the original melody 1).

Melody 4 (full retrograde)

While these may seem like academic tricks, they can be useful in creating answer phrases, countermelodies, and even entirely new themes. You must use your ears to tell you whether something "works" or not, but sometimes the use of something like retrograde can yield interesting results, those that are still connected to your original ideas. It is up to you to experiment. Perhaps you'd like to have a melody played at the same time as its retrograde. Try it out and see how it sounds. If it's not quite right, adjust some of the pitches and/or rhythms slightly to make it "right." Nothing is written in stone.

Inversion

One type of **inversion** deals with inverting the intervals of a melody. An interval is inverted by taking the lower of two pitches and placing it on top. For example, an E above a C is a major 3rd. If we take the C and move it above the E, the distance from E up to C is a minor 6th. Thus the inversion of a major 3rd is a minor 6th. Inversions of all major intervals will be minor intervals and vice versa. Inversions of perfect intervals yield perfect intervals, and inversions of diminished intervals are augmented intervals.

To invert a melody, we will use the same intervals between each note, but in the opposite direction. So, if we take Melody 1 from the earlier examples, from the first note, A, the next note is up a perfect 5th. In our inverted melody, we start with the same A and go down a perfect 5th. Next, instead of going down a 4th, we go up a perfect 4th, and so on. Every time we get to an A, both melodies will be on A. The following example shows the complete inverted melody, underneath the original melody.

You can invert a melody around the tonic, ensuring that this will be the same in both the original melody and the inverted line. If you invert around the tonic as was shown above, the new melody will conform at least somewhat to the same key. For example, if your phrases end on the tonic, to sound restful, the inverted phrases will also sound restful in the same places.

Again, this is another technique for developing your melodic ideas. Use this along with your ears to make thoughtful and artistic choices that work for you.

Augmentation and diminution

These are two rhythmic devices that can help in developing material. **Augmentation** simply means to augment or enlarge rhythmic values or durations of notes. If we take Melody 1 and multiply the duration of each note by four, we get the following.

This is essentially like taking Melody 1 and playing it four times as slow. What is the use of this? If we keep the tune in the original tempo, this augmented version could be played an octave higher using a string sound as a kind of background melody to a more groovin' part. This will be demonstrated shortly.

Diminution is the opposite of augmentation. Divide all note values by some constant number. Taking Melody 1 and dividing each note in half produces the following.

Fragmentation

When developing themes, it is common to isolate smaller parts (fragments) of the melody in order to promote a deeper level of variation. You might take one measure of a melody and repeat it several times in a row as a kind of ostinato. A theme that was stated earlier in the piece could be stated again, but only the first half of it. The second half could be a newly created part of the melody. This gives the listeners a chance to be drawn in by something familiar before being led away into new territory, somewhere they might not have been willing to go without the comforting aid of the familiar to serve as musical "bait." The new and unfamiliar can be shocking, scary, and even confusing, but fragmentation can maintain relationships with previously stated material. Think of it as "getting to know" the theme better. In your keyboard playing and composing in general, keep this in mind. Rather than playing an entire melody or motif the same all the time, choose a smaller part of it, then repeat and vary it. This can help create another layer and greater depth to your keyboard parts.

In the next example, a fragment of Melody 1 (the first two measures) is stated below in the right-hand part, and then measures 3–4 show a new and different half of the melody. A simple bass line has been added in the left hand to help put the melody in a more musical context. In measures 5–8, the first fragment of Melody 1 is repeated, but moves around at different transposition levels. It is also joined by the left hand, two octaves lower to help aid in the rhythmic drive.

TRACK 73

For the next example, we will take Melody 1, and develop it into a short but complete tune, using all the treatments discussed so far. In addition to these treatments, melodies and fragments may be transposed for further variation. The full band score has been included (minus drums), and each transformational technique has been labeled.

TRACK 74

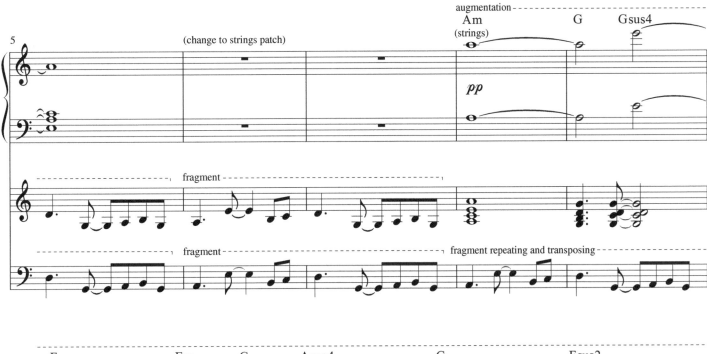

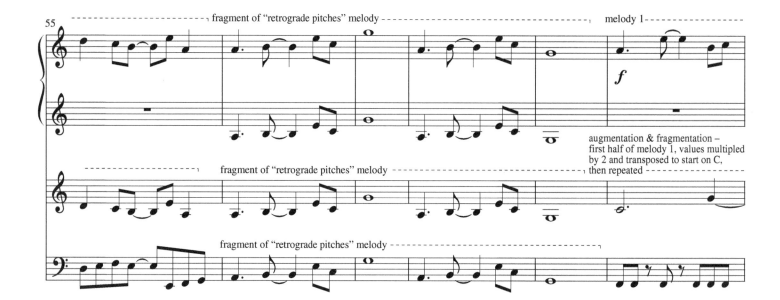

As you can see, the four-measure Melody 1 is the foundation for the entire tune. The fragments that are often utilized in this example (usually the first two measures of the theme) may be referred to as a **motif** (or **motive**). A short musical cell such as a motif, which is usually shorter than a complete theme or melody, may used over and over again to generate an entire composition. This motif may undergo treatments as shown in the previous musical example, with various forms of the motif driving or governing the entire piece. This may be referred to as **motific composition**. This technique is used in the construction of many classical works from all periods, and progressive rock often uses similar motific devices, those which take the music away from standard rock 'n' roll forms.

Regarding this example, be aware that it was created fairly "by the book," taking all the treatments literally. This can serve as a guide to help get things started, but don't think that means everything has to be written in stone. Once you've experimented with these treatments, use your imagination and creativity to shape them further, making sure they produce the musical results you really want.

Specific Forms

If you wish to create longer tunes (those not following the standard "verse–chorus" formula of pop music), and still come up with something that is solid in structure, many standard classical forms can serve as models. These are not meant to be followed strictly, in any kind of music—they are just general blueprints to help give your tunes real "plots" that makes sense. The following are just a few classical forms.

- Sonata
- Rondo
- Ternary
- Theme and Variation
- Fantasia

An entire book could be devoted to this subject. One could go through several classic prog tunes, analyze their forms, seeing if and how they fit classical models. However, in this book, we will look at a particular form, perhaps the most widely used (as well as discussed and debated about) of all classical structures, sonata form.

Sonata form

The sonata form described in the following paragraphs is one of many variations on the form. Even though it is widely used, this form is not meant to be taken literally, and many people disagree about what *sonata form* actually is. For our purposes, the form that will be described can serve as a model when beginning to compose a tune. But don't take it to mean that this is *the* definitive definition of sonata form. If you use this form as a template to start with, eventually, when inspiration and instinct drive your creative process, you may diverge from the specifics. However, in keeping with the goal of creating a kind of plot that makes sense, having this form somewhere in your considerations, and following it at least to some degree, even if loosely, will go a long way in helping to create a work that really "holds up."

We will discuss one version of sonata form, a structure with a large-scale design that consists of three main parts: **exposition**, **development**, and **recapitulation**. Sonata form (as well as other forms) may also include an **introduction** and a **coda**. These three parts (along with the intro and coda) may be referred to as the "macro design." Within each of these macro sections can be several levels of *micro* forms. The micro design is specific to each piece, and how you choose to create your own micro levels is up to you.

One of the most frequently discussed pieces in progressive rock with respect to form is "Close to the Edge" by Yes. In an article appearing in *Understanding Rock: Essays in Musical Analysis*, edited by John Covach and Graeme M. Boone (Oxford University Press, 1997), Covach gives a detailed analysis regarding the formal design of the piece, discussing how it closely resembles classical music at a structural level. The descriptions and examples below will utilize stylistic elements of "Close to the Edge" and organize them into an original composition following the common classical music structure of sonata form. It should be noted that the original "Close to the Edge" does not strictly follow sonata form, but shares many of the same structural elements, including the ways in which material is stated and developed, giving the tune more than just a superficial nod to classical music, but an emulation of it at a deeper level.

Introduction

The **introduction** can be anything—whatever you desire to start out the piece. Intros can range in length from one–two measures, to a few minutes of "setting the stage" material. In pop music, where there is great concern for tight, concise musical packages, if an intro is used at all, it is very short. Conversely, extended intros that really take the time to establish the setting and gradually bring the listener into the "world" of the tune are a hallmark of much progressive rock.

Our intro begins with a single dissonant chord that swells, leading to a rhythmic ostinato. This ostinato "groove" gives way to a *tutti* line in keys, guitar, bass, and drums to end the intro with a sustained chord.

TRACK 75

Exposition

In the **exposition**, a main theme or melody is stated as the primary element. One may think of this as the main character in a story, perhaps the protagonist. Eventually, the music heads toward establishing itself in a new key (or in non-tonal music, a new transposition level, or new pitch set/synthetic scale), either that of the dominant (from the fifth scale degree) or the relative major/minor, or even the parallel major/minor. Once the new key is established, a second theme (secondary character or antagonist) can be introduced to help stabilize it. In this new key, the secondary theme is eventually played in a cadence-like variation, i.e., something final-sounding or even semi-climactic to help bring the exposition to a close.

Example **A** picks up where the intro left off. This juncture features a chromatic mediant relationship in that the last chord of the intro, B♭ major, gives way to a D major harmony to begin the exposition. This exposition begins immediately with the main theme which is labeled "Theme A." After this theme is stated (in D major), the music would develop, gradually moving to the parallel minor, D minor. Example **B** shows the secondary theme ("Theme B"), played on the Hammond organ. This theme is divided into three parts: the first eight measures (Part I) begin in D minor. Part II of the theme is a grand statement in C major lasting only three measures. Part III includes the last four measures, and serves as a kind of "leading statement" to the next section. (These individual parts will become important later on in matters of *fragmentation*.)

On the track, the organ has been doubled with a strings patch to bring out the melody and enhance the orchestration.

TRACK 76

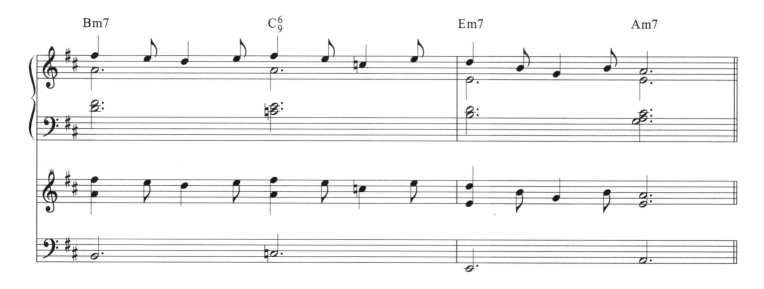

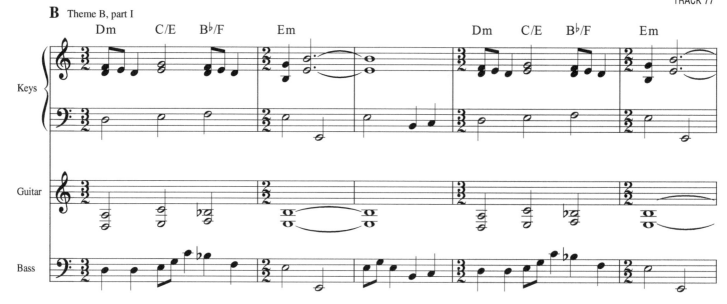

TRACK 77

B Theme B, part I

Keys

Guitar

Bass

Theme B, part II

Development

The **development** section in sonata form usually sees the first theme from the exposition sounded in various keys. In this section, this primary theme undergoes variation or manipulation. In addition to thematic variation, this section might explore a completely different mood from the first. This may be achieved through a different dynamic and tempo throughout (i.e., a very soft and atmospheric section). If the exposition was at a moderate tempo and volume, the development could be much faster and louder—whatever you feel best serves the piece and really develops the material.

In our example, Theme A is sounded in a new key during a **fugato** section. Fugatos are common in the development section in sonata form, and may be defined as a short section of imitative counterpoint within a larger work. The main subject in this fugato is the organ playing Theme A, while the bass (and guitar) play a repeated countermelody. The key is now A major, the dominant of D, which was the key of Theme A in the exposition section.

TRACK 78

One interesting development is in the rhythmic or metric treatment given to the two parts of the fugato. When isolated, Theme A (though notated differently) sounds the same as the 12/8 version from the exposition. In this setting, the theme ends up being six beats long while the bass part of the fugato is four beats in length. Theme A also begins at an odd place in time, the "and" of beat two. The "out of sync" nature of the two parts helps "thicken" the counterpoint, and represents a developmental melding of two of the different meters featured throughout the tune (the simple meter of 4/4 and the compound 12/8). Also note the added detail in the organ part: as it ends a statement of the theme on the "and" of 3 in measure 2, the left hand takes over this note, holding it out through the next sounding of the theme, an octave higher.

Continuing with the quieter, calmer mood of the exposition, Theme B will undergo some development as well. For this section, only Part II of this theme is used— an instance of fragmentation.

TRACK 79

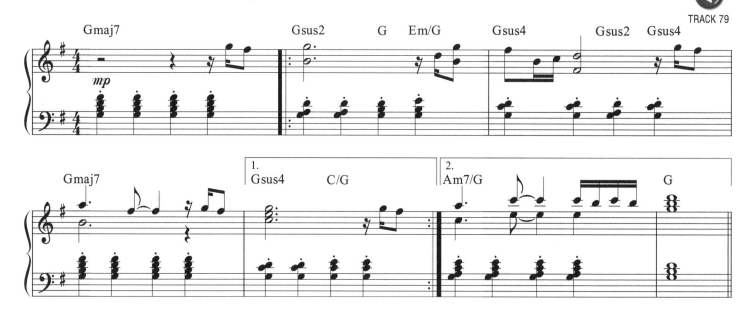

With this part of the development section, we have another change in key to G major, moving once again to a dominant relationship with the statement of Theme B (Part II) in the exposition.

Finally, the development of Theme B undergoes one last variation in the form of a grand church organ solo. The beginning motif of the development of Theme B, Part II (G–F#–G that starts off the melody above on the second sixteenth note of 4) serves as the basis for the entire pipe organ solo. This simple figure is repeated over and over, and then moves up to A♭–G–A♭, then back down to the original pitch level. The solo ends on a G major chord, setting up a kind of plagal relation (IV to I) at the return to Theme A in D major. The top note G, on the "and" of 4 is the beginning of theme A in the recapitulation section. Note that, in the recapitulation, the theme begins with a quarter note to reflect the meter change.

TRACK 80

Recapitulation

The **recapitulation** usually marks a return to the music of the exposition, including the primary theme back in its original key (or however it was sounded in the beginning: i.e., if the keyboards played the theme in the beginning, they would take over here again). This could be a literal repeat of the beginning, but some variation in some way may prove to be more interesting. In the second part of the recapitulation, where the secondary theme entered in the exposition, the secondary theme may enter again, but this time in the same key as the primary theme. Finally, a close interaction of the two themes can be effective to bring the piece to an end (or the coda, if there is one). The two themes could be played at the same time, overlapped, or could undergo a simple "back and forth."

In our example, Theme A is played at the same tempo as in the exposition, but the meter now reflects the groove played by the drums and bass, which is in 3/4. Also, instead of the simple second voice underneath the main melody, the theme is harmonized in parallel fashion at the third above for variety. Another variation occurs in that the theme is played on a Moog-like patch, instead of the organ as in the exposition.

TRACK 81

Theme A is also extended, beginning in measure 9, then played in the parallel minor, D minor (measures 13–16). This can prove to be an effective variation on any theme: if the melody is in a major key, restate it in the parallel minor, and vice-versa. The melody is still recognizable as being the same theme, but (back to the "character in a story" analogy) it is as if this same character is in a different mood for some reason.

As described above, in the recapitulation, the secondary theme is usually stated in the same key as the primary theme, whereas they were in different keys in the exposition. In our example, we stated Theme B in the parallel minor of Theme A during the exposition (D major–D minor). So now, to put Theme B in the same key *signature* as Theme A, it will be stated in the *relative* minor (B minor) rather than the parallel. This helps form a stronger connection between the two themes here in the recapitulation. Again, formally speaking, if the two main themes of the tune may be compared to characters in a story, the exposition shows them in different keys, as if they are strangers who need to get to know one another. Putting them in the same key signature at the end of the tune may be symbolic of the two characters' familiarity with one another, as if they've shared experiences, and grown together.

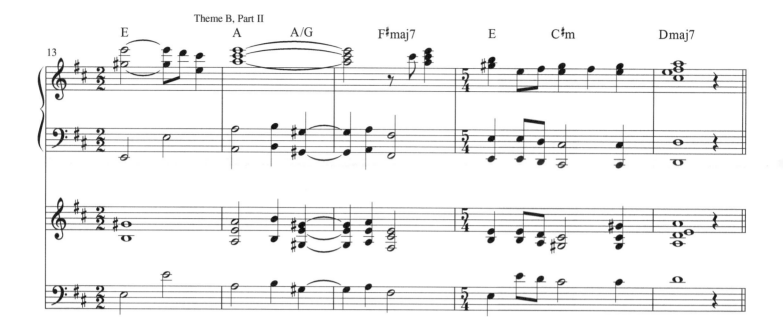

If you compare this example with Theme B as it was stated in the exposition, you will notice that the order of fragments has been changed a bit. In the exposition, we labeled the theme by three parts: I, II, and III. Here in the recapitulation, the order is now I, III, II. So besides developing individual fragments separately as a method of variation, reordering the fragments is another option.

Coda

The **coda** is an important section that can be used in any form. The word means "end" (literally, "tail") and that's what it is, an ending. Codas have been particularly prevalent in progressive rock, something to help set even more popish tunes apart from average rock 'n' roll. Like the introduction, the coda can vary in length. What is important is that it contains music that somehow constitutes the end, separating it in some way from the rest of the tune. Like in dramatic narrative, the ending could be a complete and final-sounding resolution to all the conflict that occurred within the piece. Or things can end unresolved, adding mystery and unanswered questions. A coda is also effective when it contains music that has not been heard before in the rest of the piece. Not that it should be completely unrelated, but a new surprise element can make the ending analogous to a twist at the end of a story. A piece that consists of a driving straight-rock beat all the way through could suddenly end with the main theme stated in a quiet swing style. With the recapitulation being a return to the beginning, a listener may want more than "knowing how the story will end" from this point. Even when using pop-song form, instead of ending with a fade-out chorus, add a coda. This can do wonders for any tune!

Our coda is short and simple. The piano takes up the notes of the last chord (Dmaj9) and arpeggiates them in a rhythmic pattern. This helps contrast the grandiose ending by adding something delicate that slows and quiets down, providing finality, as if the characters are reflecting on all that has transpired. However, the retention of the Dmaj9 chord along with this particular arpeggio pattern almost sounds like the beginning of a new tune. This demonstrates one example of a coda, a type that has an air of finality, yet still leaves things hanging a bit.

Conclusion

When considering this discussion of form, be sure not to let the prescriptions drive and dictate your musical creations. Use your intuition and creativity first; and then these forms can help in the refinement process to give your music a solid structure. Many musicians may compose works that end up resembling these forms, without any conscious effort to follow them. Once you have your musical ideas down in a rough sketch-like version, you can use formal concepts to "check your work," and help mold your raw ideas into something meaningful. If you are not composing the entire tune, but are working on creating your own keyboard parts for someone else's tune, you can use the concepts of repetition and variation, as well as thematic development, to give your own playing great meaning within the context of the whole tune.

Chapter 8

STYLE FILE

This chapter features six complete progressive rock tunes, composed in the style of some of the genre's most influential groups. Each of the examples represents a different sub-genre of progressive rock, and includes concepts discussed throughout the book. The audio features a full band version, as well as a play-along version with the keyboard parts left out so you can perform with the track, just like you're part of the group.

Each tune also represents varying levels of difficulty. Songs 2 and 3 are at a fairly easy level, for keyboard players at lower-intermediate stages in their technique. Songs 5 and 6 require the most advanced technique, while the remaining songs are somewhere in the middle.

1. Solar Winds (symphonic)

Summary

An ABACA (**rondo**) structure constitutes the form. In classical style, repetition and variation play an important role. The keyboard parts take advantage of multiple instruments to play the same or similar material in later sections, but with new sounds, and accompanied by new sections of music from the rest of the band.

Detail and sub-genre background

The first tune is in the style of early '70s Yes, and showcases many of the defining characteristics of symphonic progressive rock. Yes is a true icon of progressive rock, and the role of the keyboards has played a large part in establishing them as one of the giants of the genre. At the group's beginnings in the late '60s, their keyboard player, Tony Kaye stuck mainly to Hammond organ and piano as his instruments of choice. In 1971 Rick Wakeman joined the group, helping to widen the band's sonic pallet by using Mellotron, various synthesizers, organ, two or more pianos, and electric harpsichord. His contributions in instrumentation helped to bring the group's sound into the symphonic realm. Characteristic of his playing was a propensity to switch from one keyboard to another rather quickly, thereby acting as a kind of mini orchestra himself.

"Solar Winds" attempts to portray Rick Wakeman's use of Hammond organ, Mellotron strings, piano, and lead synth/Moog-like sounds and instruments. The organ is featured in the beginning of the tune, making its first statement in the form of dissonant chords in measures 2 and 4, followed by a rhythmic motif, joining the bass and guitar in measure 5. The orchestral sound enters in measure 18 with the Mellotron strings providing a lush texture that builds through measures 18–29. Harmonically, this progression makes use of suspended chords in the form of quartal sonorities (chords based on 4ths) that resolve temporarily before going on to another suspended harmony. Besides the rising motion of the chords, the harmony helps to provide tension, leading to a new section. When the driving music from the beginning returns at measure 30, the same chord progression and voicing is sounded again (measures 32–37), but this time in the organ. Though the notes are a literal repetition of what was played earlier, the instrument/sound used, and what the rest of the band is playing creates an artful variation.

In measure 45, the music takes a turn to a more pop-like song style. The piano plays a simple progression in a lilting 3/4 meter, perfect for accompanying vocals, and a nice change in instrumental color from the previous Hammond and Mellotron sounds. The organ returns, playing an arpeggio-based pattern in measures 65–70, preceded by two measures of lead-in (measures 63–64). The Mellotron soon follows, playing another type of rising gesture based on suspended harmonies in measures 72–75. Again we see a repetition of material from earlier, but used in a new way, within a different musical setting.

Boldly announcing its entrance, the Moog synth plays a syncopated pattern in parallel harmony with the guitar in measures 76–81. Not only is the musical gesture itself a surprise in its almost "out of place" character, but the fresh synth sound helps underscore its interruptive nature, breaking up the mellower 3/4 pop-like music. This statement also serves to set up the next phrase at measure 82, which sees a return to the earlier 3/4 music, this time stated louder, with the same chord progression played on the organ.

In measure 90, another bold synth motif is introduced, bringing the keyboards firmly into the foreground. This figure is somewhat Baroque-like in dexterity, offering a classical music element. (If it were played on harpsichord, one would definitely hear the Baroque influence.) This is also the first time we see the use of an odd meter, a 7/8 with a "3+4" subdivision. The figure is used to interrupt the heavy driving music from the beginning of the tune, thereby giving the listener a surprise, and something new, rather than a predictable literal recap of earlier material. This all gives way to one more statement of the rising suspended gesture in the Mellotron to conclude the tune.

TRACK 84
full band

TRACK 85
minus keyboards

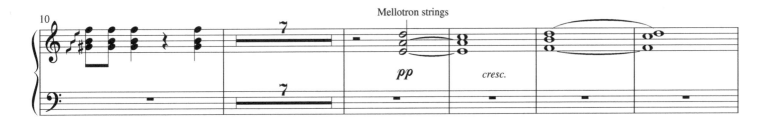

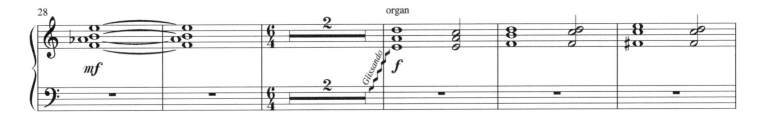

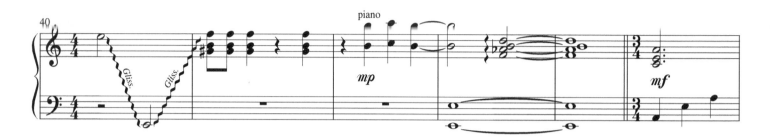

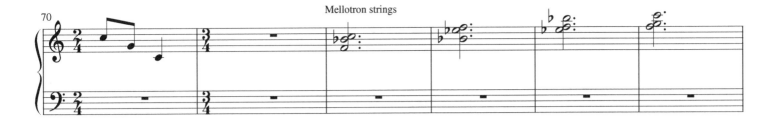

Mellotron strings

Moog

organ

Moog

organ

Moog

2. Shades of a Dream (space rock)

Summary

The form takes on a large-scale ABA (**Ternary**) structure, with the two A sections sharing only a similarity of mood and general style rather than actual musical material. There is also a short coda used to bring finality to an otherwise repetitious pattern in the final section. Most of the keyboards play in a simple homophonic manner (left-hand chords accompanying right-hand melody). Through the use of exotic scales, repetition, and simple but effective chromatic harmonic relationships, an atmosphere of mystery is created. The mood is enhanced by a contrasting middle section, played by a different instrument, adding a touch of conflict to bridge the two atmospheric sections. Effects such as reverb and delay applied in liberal amounts help enhance the moodiness of the tune, taking the listener "somewhere else," far away and imaginative.

Detail and sub-genre background

For our space rock tune we turn to one of the founders of the sub-genre, Pink Floyd. With this style, an emphasis was placed on atmosphere. Unlike other rock 'n' roll, this music was not specifically designed for dancing or partying, nor did it rely heavily upon strong **hooks** (catchy, singable melodies). In a lot of classical-based prog, much of the attention went to virtuosic playing—great displays of instrumental (and vocal) technique. But here, with space rock, there is an emphasis on mood. One may think of it as the setting of a story, minus the characters and action. A listener can relax, enjoy, and be taken to this imaginary land through the music.

In the first section of "Shades of a Dream," the keyboard melody is played with a soft, reed-like organ setting, adding a considerable amount of reverb for atmosphere. The left hand follows the repetitive accompaniment, alternating back and forth between E5 and G5 chords (root and 5th only, no 3rd), playing these sonorities with Mellotron strings. The right-hand melody uses pitches from the **double harmonic** scale, related to the harmonic minor scale, which you learned in Chapter 6. This scale contains *two* augmented 2nds between the second and third and sixth and seventh degrees, adding to the exotic sound. With the E chord, an E double harmonic scale is used: E, F, G#, A, B, C, D#, E. With the G chord, the G double harmonic scale is used: G, Ab, B, C, D, Eb, F#, G. Notice how the two scales have only four pitches in common: G#/Ab, B, C, and Eb/D#. In the E scale, the third degree is G#, thus a move to the scale based on G natural, a pitch not part of the E scale, shows a kind of chromatic mediant relationship as discussed in

Chapter 4. Even though we have a simple and repetitive pattern in this alternation between only two chords, it is the lack of commonality between the two chords (and the scales that go with them) that helps produce this "far out" sound. This is highly characteristic of psychedelic music—utilizing a great degree of repetition with a small amount of musical material (only two chords), yet choosing elements that, though ordinary by themselves, sound exotic when combined together or played "side by side."

The middle section sees a change in instrumentation and mood. The piano is used (a highly percussive instrument, especially when compared with the smooth and lyrical character of the previous organ melody and Mellotron strings) to provide for a more tense, agitated section. This section serves as the "conflict" within the music. If we think of this like a story, the first section presents the setting, where things are calm and serene. As in most stories, things never stay nice and calm for long—a problem of some sort must arise, demanding a solution. With the damper pedal down, the piano plays a series of violent clusters utilizing the entire palm surface of the hand. When the last notes of this conflict echo into the distance, the conflict is over, and the answer to the "problem" of the story ushers in the final section.

In this part of the tune, we see a return to a more serene style, but played over a more "grooving" accompaniment. In much psychedelic music, with a desire to conjure up hallucinogenic and surreal imagery, there was perhaps no greater effect used than the **delay** (which causes the sound to echo, repeating itself, but dying away in volume). This effect could be applied to any instrument, and when used to a considerable degree, the sounds of the instrument would be transformed instantly into something "spacey," not quite grounded on this earth. Even "non-musical" sounds can be turned into psychedelic sonorities by applying delay. Something as everyday as the sound of tearing a piece of paper could have delay applied to it, and thus become part of "space music." In our tune, the right hand plays a simple Moog solo which is greatly enhanced by delay. The left hand sustains chords in the organ, much as the left hand did with the Mellotron in the first section.

TRACK 86
full band

TRACK 87
minus keyboards

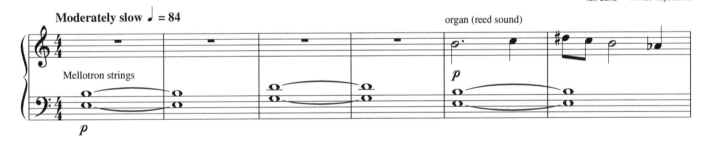

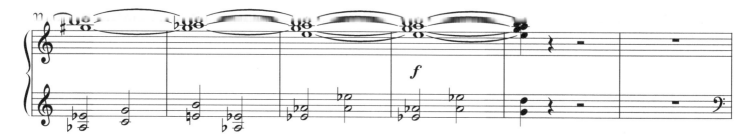

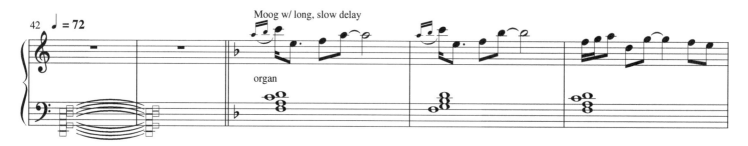

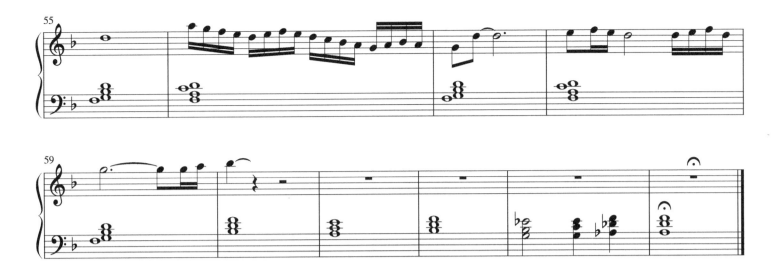

3. *Within the Lines* (neoprogressive)

Summary

The ABCAB+coda form gives the listener standard pop-song repeats, but adds the all-important coda at the end to hold the listener's interest all the way through. Keyboards play a two-handed part, with basic chords in the right hand while the left hand often doubles the bass. The music is varied by presenting similar material in different time signatures. Apart from chords, the right hand plays a lead synth solo in the middle for melodic contrast.

Detail and sub-genre background

Though Rush was clearly in the progressive vein in the '70s, the '80s saw the trio adapting with the times, creating shorter, more refined rock songs. Rush also exemplified the guitar-driven, hard rock side of the neo progressive style, with leanings toward heavy metal. It is no surprise that their music has thus influenced many of the groups in the progressive metal genre. As far as the role of the keyboards was concerned, the quaint analog synth solos of the '70s were replaced by a thicker digital symphonic sound, often serving as background, or adding orchestrational details. Still, there were some keyboard-driven tunes, and this example represents the keyboard-based style of '80s Rush.

This tune uses a layered synth brass and strings patch, with both hands playing most of the time. Since Rush's keyboardist was also the group's bass player, the left hand serves a very important role, playing a solid rhythmic bass line. The right hand plays the tune's primary motif, outlining its chord structure in the verse sections. The middle section (beginning at measure 37) sees a soloistic keyboard melody, a remnant from the keyboard melodies that played a major role in their '70s classics. The patch is changed on the keyboard to a more analog "lead-type" sound to help distinguish it from the rest of the keyboard parts. We also see Rush's trademark meter changes and odd meter. At measure 13, the opening motif continues, but this time with a solid quarter-note pulse, alternating with 7/8. We've seen this type of metric variation before where a melody or phrase is stated two ways, once in an odd meter, and then slightly altered to fit into an even meter. Such details showcase the "prog" nature, adding the extra bit of artistic variation to the repetition. Notice the repeat map of the tune, which asks for literal repeats of certain sections, indicative of the more pop-rock style, thus exemplifying the neoprogressive sub-genre.

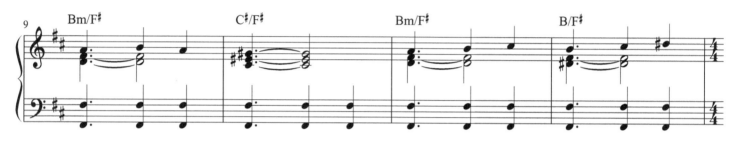

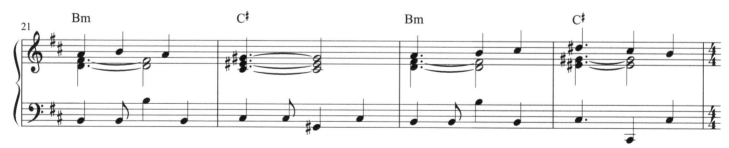

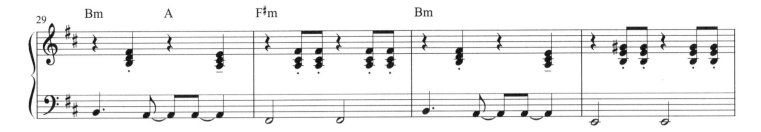

To Coda ⊕

Patch change to lead synth

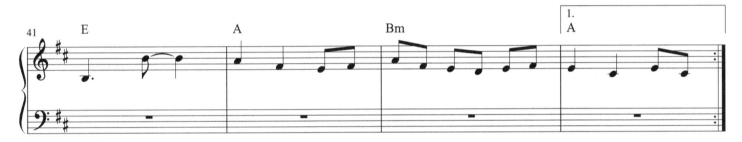

D.S. al Coda

Patch change to original

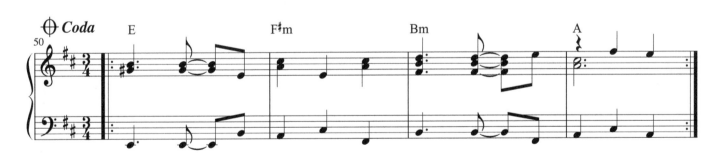

⊕ *Coda*

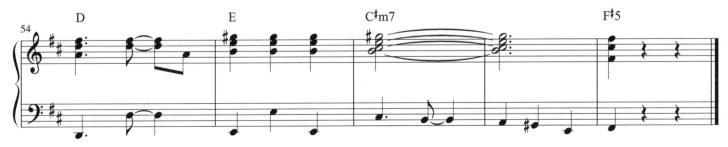

4. *Revenge of the Insects* (Rock in Opposition)

Summary

The form follows an intro+ABABC+coda structure with the C section acting more as a short bridge. The coda provides a dramatic contrast in musical material via a sharp change in meter and rhythmic style, acting as an all-important release to the drone-like repetitions that precede it—exemplary of a true coda in its "surprise ending" character. A minimal amount of material is used in the form of two cluster chords and ostinato figures that undergo variation to keep the music progressing.

Detail and sub-genre background

The harmonic structure of this tune takes on many of the characteristics found in Chapter 4 under "atonality." The piece is in the style of the Belgian group Univers Zero, one of the original RIO groups who took heavy influence from composers like Stravinsky and Bartók as well as the minimalist composers from the latter part of the twentieth-century. In listening to the audio, notice the dissonant harmony and the very "non-rock" drumming, characteristic of this style of progressive rock. The tune also represents the "chamber rock" stylings in that is uses no synthesizers (only piano) and includes cello instead of guitar.

The entire tune is based on the pitches of an octatonic scale (C, C#, D#, E, F#, G, A, B♭), a common source of pitch material used by Stravinsky and Bartók. The piano part opens with a dissonant chord consisting of three notes containing the intervals of a minor 2nd between the bottom two, a perfect 4th between the top two, and a tritone between the outer two. Though made up of three pitches, this is clearly not a major, minor, augmented, or diminished triad. A very similar chord follows, containing the same two intervals of a minor second and tritone. Its perfect 5th is actually an inversion of the first chord's perfect 4th, making the chords sound essentially the same. For the purposes of this discussion, these two chords *will* be considered the same, referred to as "chord 1." There is one more basic chord used in this tune, a slightly more open and less dissonant sonority, yet similar to the previous chords. In measure 6, the harmony includes the intervals of the major 2nd, minor 6th, and again the tritone. We will call this sonority "chord 2." These two chords are repeated at various transposition levels throughout, with occasional inversions of the intervals. These dissonant harmonies are characteristic of **post tonal** classical music, while the repetition of only two basic chords throughout an entire tune is a nod toward minimalism.

Perhaps the most noticeable use of repetition occurs in the ostinato commencing in measure 15, played by the cello. Also note the slightly contrasting ostinato in the percussion.

Subtle orchestrational variations color the ostinato. On the track, you will notice the bass part playing only bits of the ostinato in unison with the cello, gradually increasing its role until it plays the full pattern.

Melodic interest begins in the piano part in measure 23. The melody uses pitches and intervals from chord 2, and undergoes slight variation each time it is played. Sometimes the melody is doubled in the left hand, an octave below (measures 25–26). The melody also varies in length, sometimes sounding fragmented.

The **B** section features a new ostinato consisting of a reversal of the rhythm between the cello/bass and percussion parts. The piano part diverts from the melody in a return to playing chords as it did earlier.

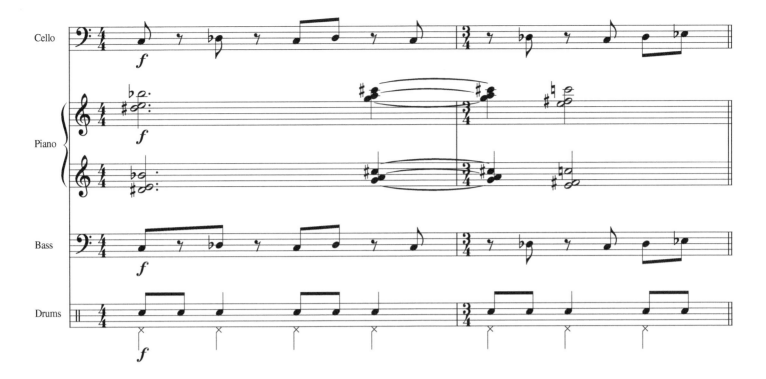

As the repetitions build in intensity, some sort of release is demanded. This is achieved only in the coda with a shift in tempo and meter—perhaps the insects referred to in the title finally have gathered together in a swarm to enact their revenge. The pulse of the music remains the same in the coda, as indicated by the "♩ = ♩·" marking. With the dotted quarter now representing the pulse, each beat, though the same tempo as before, is divided into three as shown in the driving and repetitious piano figure. A regular alternation between the hands can help keep this even, but be aware that each group of three notes begins with a different hand. Practice by accenting slightly the first and fourth of each group of six eighth notes (right, left, right, left, right, left, etc.)

TRACK 90
full band

TRACK 91
minus keyboards

Coda

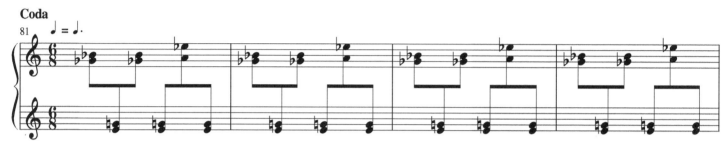

5. *Fortress* (progressive metal)

Summary

This tune is filled with all the elements of classic progressive rock, along with several important prog metal characteristics. Meter changes and odd meters help add an element of unpredictability. Though the tune begins in B minor, with each new section, this tonality is stretched until a more fully chromatic palette emerges for the ending melodies and motifs. True to the prog metal style that Dream Theater helped invent, fast scalar-based solo lines, sometimes in unison with the guitar or parallel to it characterize one of the highlights. Often these lines are given extra drive through the persistent use of the double-kick pedal in the drumset, a real prog metal staple. You may also notice that this tune is almost exclusively for the right hand. The left hand is free to control the pitch bend and vibrato wheel/stick should you wish to enhance your playing with these embellishments

Detail and sub-genre background

In the 1980s most progressive rock existed "underground," no longer in the mainstream. There were lots of new bands forming, recording albums and playing live, but outside the cadre of dedicated fans that helped keep the movement alive, the genre was considered a thing of the past. Eventually, a handful of heavy metal and speed metal groups took influence from the founding groups of the '70s, incorporating many of the classic prog elements into their heavy metal. The earliest of the groups included Watchtower, Sieges Even, Fates Warning, and Dream Theater. Among these bands, Dream Theater was the first really to break into mainstream rock, helping to bring a little bit of prog back into the "charts." Their second album, *Images and Words*, received commercial radio play and MTV video broadcast. The group showcased all the progressive rock elements discussed in this book, along with the heavy metal trademark distortion-driven rhythm guitars and liberal use of the double kick drums. Virtuosic keyboards really helped to set progressive metal apart from other heavy/speed metal.

This tune was composed in the style of Dream Theater, and the keyboard parts are largely in a melodic and soloistic style. The beginning sees a simple, repetitive part, but one with a small "trick" to it. With the meter changing back and forth from 3/4 to 7/8, it is important to notice *where* in the measure the chord is sounded. Though a chord is played on every quarter-note throughout the first eight bars, the 7/8 meter puts the notes on the off-beats in the second 3/4 measure. This "playing with time" aspect adds an element of distinctiveness to the simple part. When playing this, and other similar gestures, stay rigid in your timing: tapping eighth notes in your foot can help keep this together.

Measure 9 sees a break from the chords with the playing of a melody. Notice by listening to the audio that this melody is sounded in parallel harmony with the guitar, a Dream Theater trademark.

The music erupts into a fast scalar passage beginning in measure 17, this time in unison with the guitar. Though this may sound difficult, what is played here is a familiar D major scale. If you practice all of the major (and minor, etc.) scales, a run like this will be perfected in no time.

After some bridging material, the tune launches into another soloistic, run-based section at measure 39. Where earlier we saw one line in parallel harmony with the guitar, and then another in unison with it, this solo combines both elements. Though the guitar and keyboard begin in unison, they break apart into parallelism at certain moments. When practicing parts like this, it is best to get with your guitar player and play these lines together, at a slower tempo, with a metronome. This will ensure that you stay tightly together when joining the full band, up to tempo. This section also shifts to the dominant of the original B minor key; as we are now in F♯ major. Though clearly not a blues-based rock 'n' roll tune, hints of the rock roots surface in the blues scale application to the solo in measures 51–52. Here, the flatted third and fifth scale degrees (A♮ and C♮) add a bit of a blues lick to this otherwise diatonic major section.

The harmonic character takes another turn via the keyboard motif in measures 55–58. Though still under a tonic of F♯, a return to the pitches of the B minor/D major scale put this melody in the F♯ Phrygian mode.

The gradual stretch of tonality continues as the music elaborates the original B minor in measures 59–70. Here the main motif alternates between B minor and C (no third is present, so it could be C major or C minor). To enhance the effect of this motif, the keys are joined by both guitar and bass, all playing the figure in unison.

In measures 71–82, the tonality stretches further with some increased chromaticism. Short rising gestures utilizing the chromatic scale are played over an E–F pedal figure in the guitar and bass (similar to the B–C motif from the previous section). The left hand enters to complement the right in measure 77, filling in the rhythmic gaps in the right-hand part. The chromatic figures continue in measure 83, this time with a return to the full band in unison, helping to build the intensity.

Finally, in the most symphonic moment of the tune, the keys play string-section stabs in syncopated rhythms beginning in measure 99, bringing the tune to a climactic close.

TRACK 92
full band

TRACK 93
minus keyboards

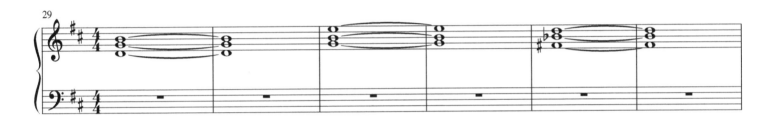

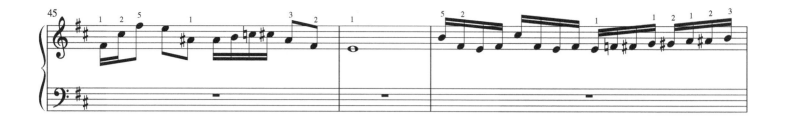

6. Welcome 2 the Show (classical)

Summary

Though this music hints at elements of pop song forms, the use of multiple interludes, and considerable variation of repeated material are taken from classical methods of composition. Repeating sections in a parallel key (the first verse in A minor, to the second in A major) is also a common classical method of variation.

Detail and sub-genre background

This tune is in the style of early '70s ELP, and is a large-scale work requiring considerable keyboard chops. It is one of the most advanced songs in the Style File, showing one of the highlights of prog keyboard players—virtuosity. However, this tune can also be used as a model for form and compositional technique in creating your own keyboard parts at any level of difficulty.

In the introduction, we hear an example of fugal/imitative counterpoint, used in a typical Baroque manner. The first subject (melody) begins in the right hand, and then two measures later, as it continues, the left hand enters in imitation, producing two of the same basic melodies, sounded two measures out of sync with each other. Although the key of A minor is indicated, the fugal subject is more of an A blues, thus putting a bit of rock 'n' roll into this very Baroque opening.

Once the solo organ fugue is finished, the full band kicks in, with the organ playing in more of a chordal style (measure 9) to start the verse. Measures 11–12 consist of a **bridge phrase**—a short gesture used to connect other phrases together. This bridge recurs regularly throughout this section. In measures 17–18, the right hand plays a simple rhythmic motif on the organ while the left hand plays a bass line in the low register of the piano. Note that, for this part of the verse, the electric bass in the band drops out, placing great importance on the keyboards to fill the bass role. The low piano continues in the second part of the verse (now joined by the electric bass), while the right hand recalls the bridge phrase. The verse ends with a kind of tail played in octaves using the Moog sound. Although performance on two or three keyboards would be ideal, it is easy enough on most synthesizers to put the keyboard into split mode—the upper half of the keyboard would be assigned an organ patch, and the left hand, piano. When the Moog phrase comes in at measure 25, one would have to change patches quickly. Again, this is a skill that prog keyboardists must practice. Alternatively, many keyboards have the option of using a foot switch for patch changes, making this easier. Experiment with what works best for you.

Measures 28–38 consist of an instrumental interlude utilizing the theme from the very beginning, stated here in measure 30. This time the left hand accompanies the melody with an ascending scalar run rather than the imitation seen in the intro: repetition with variation.

The next section (measures 39–50) goes into a shuffle feel and features a right hand-only Moog solo. The section is set up by a D7 chord in measure 38, promoting an expectation that the solo will begin in G. Thus, the C major start to the section is a surprise, breaking the "rules" of tonality. However, the diversion is only temporary as the solo section soon settles down on a solid G, three measures into it.

Although Verse 2 begins the same as Verse 1, an abrupt change is made in measure 59, where the tune goes into the parallel key of A major. As if spurred by this new brighter key, the tempo also speeds up, and the hands are again divided between the classic Moog melody in the right and the chordal organ in the left.

In Interlude II, it is as if the new major key helped inspire new musical material. A typical prog odd meter helps support a new theme in the right hand. When playing in 7/8, it is important to note how this compound meter is divided. In this case, the 3+4 subdivision establishes the overall rhythmic feel and can help things stay tightly together. The first part of the measure is syncopated (a two dotted eighth-note rhythm), while the second part is made up of four even eighths. Use these even eighth notes to help lock into the feel of this odd meter. In measure 91, we return to 4/4 with a right-hand fanfare statement in the Moog, and the organ figures answering each call. When playing the glissando passage in measures 98–99, remember that the pitches are approximate. Don't play this two "neatly": a kind of rough and aggressive approach is desired. The left hand will play the final glissando, preparing the right hand to return to the Moog melody.

Verse 3 remains in A major, and sees a simpler version of Verse 2—this time utilizing only the I, IV, and V chords: very rock 'n' roll. The verse takes a turn in measure 104 as a virtuosic flourish gives way to a rising gesture to end the verse. The section ends with a similar statement to that of Verse 2, but this time, because we've heard this chord before, it is only sounded for a fraction of the duration.

Just like after Verse 2, Verse 3 goes into the same type of interlude, here labeled "Interlude III"— this is the same but shorter (again, we've heard this already, so a shorter statement is desired). The descending scalar figure from Interlude II (measure 90) recurs in Interlude III, now extended to lead into the coda where a new type of rhythmic gesture, sounded in dissonant stacks (basically ♭5 triads, doubling the flatted fifth) presents a sound of climactic finality.

Intro

♩ = 144

Organ

Verse 1

Interlude 1

Shuffle

Verse 2
Straight eighths

Suddenly Faster ♩ = 168

Moog

organ

Interlude 2

♪ = 232 3+4

Moog

organ

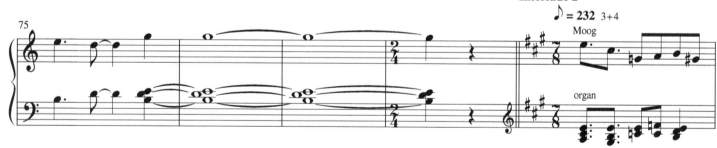

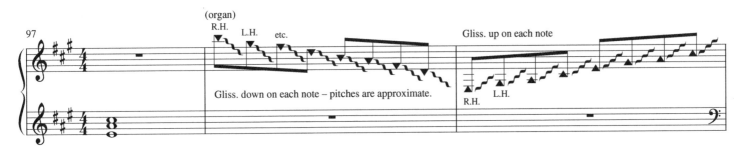

Verse 3

Interlude 3

Coda